PENGUIN BOOKS — GREAT FOOD

Love in a Dish and Other Pieces

MARY FRANCES KENNEDY FISHER (1908–1992) is considered one of the greatest American food writers of the twentieth century. In 1929, the newly married Fisher travelled with her husband to Dijon, in France, where she tasted real French cooking for the first time and learned how to live and eat well and economically. She returned in 1932 to an American appetite weakened by the Great Depression and began to write essays of her own. The author of many books, including the wartime classic *How to Cook a Wolf*, she aimed always to inspire cooks and combined recipes with reflection, anecdote and passionate storytelling. Considered the 'poet of the appetites' by John Updike, and hailed by W. H. Auden as the greatest American prose writer, her culinary essays have become American classics.

D1513393

Love in a Dish and Other Pieces

M. F. K. FISHER

Chosen by Anne Zimmerman

PENGUIN BOOKS

PENGUIN BOOKS

Published by the Penguin Group
Penguin Books Ltd, 80 Strand, London WC2R 0RL, England
Penguin Group (USA) Inc., 375 Hudson Street, New York, New York 10014, USA
Penguin Group (Canada), 90 Eglinton Avenue East, Suite 700, Toronto, Ontario,
Canada M4P 2Y3 (a division of Pearson Penguin Canada Inc.)
Penguin Ireland, 25 St Stephen's Green, Dublin 2, Ireland
(a division of Penguin Books Ltd)
Penguin Group (Australia), 250 Camberwell Road,
Camberwell, Victoria 3124, Australia
(a division of Pearson Australia Group Pty Ltd)
Penguin Books India Pvt Ltd, 11 Community Centre,
Panchsheel Park, New Delhi – 110 017, India
Penguin Group (NZ), 67 Apollo Drive, Rosedale, Auckland 0632, New Zealand
(a division of Pearson New Zealand Ltd)
Penguin Books (South Africa) (Pty) Ltd, 24 Sturdee Avenue,
Rosebank, Johannesburg 2196, South Africa

Penguin Books Ltd, Registered Offices: 80 Strand, London WC2R 0RL, England

www.penguin.com

This collection published in Penguin Books 2011
This edition published for The Book People Ltd, 2011
Hall Wood Avenue, Haydock, St Helens, WA11 9UL

1

Copyright © M. F. K. Fisher, c/o Robert Lescher, Trustee of the Literary Trust
All rights reserved

Cover design based on a pattern from a Century design side plate by Eva Zeisel for
Hallcraft, 1957. Transfer-printed earthenware. (Photograph copyright © Victoria &
Albert Museum.) Picture research by Samantha Johnson. Lettering by Stephen Raw

Set in 10.75/13pt Berkeley Oldstyle Book
Typeset by Jouve (UK), Milton Keynes
Printed in Great Britain by Clays Ltd, St Ives plc

ISBN 978-0-241-96085-1

www.greenpenguin.co.uk

Contents

Sources

Uncle Evans

Uncle Evans was my mother's favorite brother and perhaps my father's favorite man friend, and he was my favorite relative because he was worthy of all this family worship. He liked us, too, and spent many of his sabbaticals near us, writing unread law books. When I was eighteen he suggested, to my astonishment, that we travel together from California to Chicago, where he would go on eastward to his university post and I would go south to a small college. I now believe that he did this on purpose, to help me into new worlds.

It was my first train trip of more than three hours. I was dazed at escaping the family nest. My clothes were correctly navy-blue *crepe de chine* (because of the soot), and I slept in the upper berth because I was younger than my uncle. I spent most of my time on the observation platform or in the ladies' room washing my hands. We met for lunch and dinner.

Uncle Evans was a seasoned commuter between West and East from the turn of the century until about 1940. He even had special clothes made for those gritty but delicious 'trips,' as they were always called: odd-looking three-piece suits made of 'dirt-proof' alpaca or something. (Only white shirts, of course, with starched collars: he was a *professor*.) The trains were good. He knew them.

He knew the conductors and porters and dining stewards. He even knew the engineer.

In those days (1927 for my maiden voyage), the trains stopped often, and there were still a few Harvey Houses along the line. ('The only test of a good breakfast place is its baked apple,' Uncle Evans said mildly. 'The Harvey girls never fail me.') One time Uncle Evans walked me up to the engine at a desolate stop, and we stayed too long and were hauled up bodily into the cab until the next slowdown. It was exciting. And there were still prairie-dog huts along the track and conelike ovens in the westward country, in silent ugly Americanized villages that still dared not tell the Indians what kind of bread to bake.

As an old hand, Uncle Evans knew where to ask the dining-car steward to put on things like live trout, venison, fresh corn, melons. They were served to him at our twinkling, snowy little table in the restaurant car, at noon and at night, and I paddled along happily in the small sensual spree my uncle always made of his routine travelings. I probably heard and felt and tasted more than either of us could be aware of.

One time when he looked at me over his menu and asked me whether I would like something like a fresh mushroom omelet or one with wild asparagus, and I mumbled in my shy ignorance that I really did not care, he put down the big information sheet and for one of the few times in my life with him, he spoke a little sharply. He said, 'You should never say that again, dear girl. It is stupid, which you are not. It implies that the attentions of your host are basically wasted on you. So make up your mind, before you open your mouth. Let him believe, even if it is a lie, that you would infinitely prefer the exotic wild asparagus to the banal mushrooms, or vice versa. Let him feel that it matters to you . . . and even that *he* does!

'All this,' my uncle added gently, 'may someday teach you about the art of seduction, as well as the more important art of knowing yourself.' Then he turned to the waiter and ordered two wild asparagus omelets. I wanted for a minute, I still remember, to leave the dining car and weep a little in the sooty ladies' room, but instead I stayed there and suddenly felt more secure and much wiser – always a heady experience but especially so at nineteen. And I don't believe that since then I have ever said, 'I don't care,' when I am offered a choice of any kind of food and drink. As Uncle Evans pointed out to me, I either care or I'm a dolt, and dolts should not consort with caring people.

I was Really Very Hungry

I

Once I met a young servant in northern Burgundy who was almost frighteningly fanatical about food, like a medieval woman possessed by a devil. Her obsession engulfed even my appreciation of the dishes she served, until I grew uncomfortable.

It was the off season at the old mill which a Parisian chef had bought and turned into one of France's most famous restaurants, and my mad waitress was the only servant. In spite of that she was neatly uniformed, and showed no surprise at my unannounced arrival and my hot dusty walking clothes.

She smiled discreetly at me, said, 'Oh, but certainly!' when I asked if I could lunch there, and led me without more words to a dark bedroom bulging with First Empire furniture, and a new white bathroom.

When I went into the dining room it was empty of humans – a cheerful ugly room still showing traces of the petit bourgeois parlor it had been. There were aspidistras on the mantel; several small white tables were laid with those imitation 'peasant-ware' plates that one sees in Paris china stores, and very good crystal glasses; a cat folded under some ferns by the window ledge hardly looked at me; and the air was softly hurried with the sound of high waters from the stream outside.

I waited for the maid to come back. I knew I should eat well and slowly, and suddenly the idea of dry sherry, unknown in all the village bistros of the last few days, stung my throat smoothly. I tried not to think of it; it would be impossible to realize. Dubonnet would do. But not as well. I longed for sherry.

The little maid came into the silent room. I looked at her stocky young body, and her butter-colored hair, and noticed her odd pale voluptuous mouth before I said, 'Mademoiselle, I shall drink an apéritif. Have you by any chance –'

'Let me suggest,' she interrupted firmly, 'our special dry sherry. It is chosen in Spain for Monsieur Paul.'

And before I could agree she was gone, discreet and smooth.

She's a funny one, I thought, and waited in a pleasant warm tiredness for the wine.

It was good. I smiled approval at her, and she lowered her eyes, and then looked searchingly at me again. I realized suddenly that in this land of trained nonchalant waiters I was to be served by a small waitress who took her duties seriously. I felt much amused, and matched her solemn searching gaze.

'Today, Madame, you may eat shoulder of lamb in the English style, with baked potatoes, green beans, and a sweet.'

My heart sank. I felt dismal, and hot and weary, and still grateful for the sherry.

But she was almost grinning at me, her lips curved triumphantly, and her eyes less palely blue.

'Oh, in *that* case,' she remarked as if I had spoken, 'in *that* case a trout, of course – a *truite au bleu* as only Monsieur Paul can prepare it!'

She glanced hurriedly at my face, and hastened on. 'With the trout, one or two young potatoes – oh, very delicately boiled,' she added before I could protest, 'very light.'

I felt better. I agreed. 'Perhaps a leaf or two of salad after the fish,' I suggested. She almost snapped at me. 'Of course, of course! And naturally our hors d'oeuvres to commence.' She started away.

'No!' I called, feeling that I must assert myself now or be forever lost. 'No!'

She turned back, and spoke to me very gently. 'But Madame has never tasted our hors d'oeuvres. I am sure that Madame will be pleased. They are our specialty, made by Monsieur Paul himself. I am sure,' and she looked reproachfully at me, her mouth tender and sad, 'I am sure that Madame would be very much pleased.'

I smiled weakly at her, and she left. A little cloud of hurt gentleness seemed to hang in the air where she had last stood.

I comforted myself with the sherry, feeling increasing irritation with my own feeble self. Hell! I loathed hors d'oeuvres! I conjured disgusting visions of square glass plates of oily fish, of soggy vegetables glued together with cheap mayonnaise, of rank radishes and tasteless butter. No, Monsieur Paul or not, sad young pale-faced waitress or not, I hated hors d'oeuvres.

I glanced victoriously across the room at the cat, whose eyes seemed closed.

II

Several minutes passed. I was really very hungry.

The door banged open, and my girl came in again, less discreet this time. She hurried toward me.

'Madame, the wine! Before Monsieur Paul can go on –' Her eyes watched my face, which I perversely kept rather glum.

'I think,' I said ponderously, daring her to interrupt me, 'I think that today, since I am in Burgundy and about to eat a trout,' and here I hoped she noticed that I did not mention hors d'oeuvres, 'I think I shall drink a bottle of Chablis 1929.'

For a second her whole face blazed with joy, and then subsided into a trained mask. I knew that I had chosen well, had somehow satisfied her in a secret and incomprehensible way. She nodded politely and scuttled off, only for another second glancing impatiently at me as I called after her, 'Well cooled, please, but not iced.'

I'm a fool, I thought, to order a whole bottle. I'm a fool, here all alone and with more miles to walk before I reach Avallon and my fresh clothes and a bed. Then I smiled at myself and leaned back in my solid wide-seated chair, looking obliquely at the prints of Gibson girls, English tavern scenes, and hideous countrysides that hung on the papered walls. The room was warm; I could hear my companion cat purring under the ferns.

The girl rushed in, with flat baking dishes piled up

her arms like the plates of a Japanese juggler. She slid them off neatly in two rows onto the table, where they lay steaming up at me, darkly and infinitely appetizing.

'*Mon Dieu!* All for me?' I peered at her. She nodded, her discretion quite gone now and a look of ecstatic worry on her pale face and eyes and lips.

There were at least eight dishes. I felt almost embarrassed, and sat for a minute looking weakly at the fork and spoon in my hand.

'Perhaps Madame would care to start with the pickled herring? It is not like any other. Monsieur Paul prepares it himself, in his own vinegar and wines. It is very good.'

I dug out two or three brown filets from the dish, and tasted. They were truly unlike any others, truly the best I had ever eaten, mild, pungent, meaty as fresh nuts.

I realized the maid had stopped breathing, and looked up at her. She was watching me, or rather a gastronomic X ray of the herring inside me, with a hypnotized glaze in her eyes.

'Madame is pleased?' she whispered softly.

I said I was. She sighed, and pushed a sizzling plate of broiled endive toward me, and disappeared.

I had put a few dull green lentils on my plate, lentils scattered with minced fresh herbs and probably marinated in tarragon vinegar and walnut oil, when she came into the dining room again with the bottle of Chablis in a wine basket.

'Madame should be eating the little baked onions while they are hot,' she remarked over her shoulder as she held the bottle in a napkin and uncorked it. I obeyed meekly, and while I watched her I ate several more than I had meant to. They were delicious, simmered first in strong meat broth, I think, and then drained and broiled with olive oil and new-ground pepper.

I was fascinated by her method of uncorking a vintage wine. Instead of the Burgundian procedure of infinite and often exaggerated precautions against touching or tipping or jarring the bottle, she handled it quite nonchalantly, and seemed to be careful only to keep her hands from the cool bottle itself, holding it sometimes by the basket and sometimes in a napkin. The cork was very tight, and I thought for a minute that she would break it. So did she: her face grew tight, and did not loosen until she had slowly worked out the cork and wiped the lip. Then she poured an inch of wine in a glass, turned her back to me like a priest taking Communion, and drank it down. Finally some was poured for me, and she stood with the bottle in her hand and her full lips drooping until I nodded a satisfied yes. Then she pushed another of the plates toward me, and almost rushed from the room.

I ate slowly, knowing that I should not be as hungry as I ought to be for the trout, but knowing too that I had never tasted such delicate savory morsels. Some were hot, some cold. The wine was light and cool. The room, warm and agreeably empty under the rushing sound of the stream, became smaller as I grew used to it.

My girl hurried in again, with another row of plates up one arm, and a large bucket dragging at the other. She slid the plates deftly onto the table, and drew a deep breath as she let the bucket down against the table leg.

'Your trout, Madame,' she said excitedly. I looked down at the gleam of the fish curving through its limited water. 'But first a good slice of Monsieur Paul's *pâté*. Oh yes, oh yes, you will be very sorry if you miss this. It is rich, but appetizing, and not at all too heavy. Just this one morsel!'

And willy-nilly I accepted the large gouge she dug from a terrine. I prayed for ten normal appetites and thought with amused nostalgia of my usual lunch of cold milk and fruit as I broke off a crust of bread and patted it smooth with the paste. Then I forgot everything but the exciting faint decadent flavor in my mouth.

I beamed up at the girl. She nodded, but from habit asked if I was satisfied. I beamed again, and asked, simply to please her, 'Is there not a faint hint of *marc*, or perhaps cognac?'

'*Marc*, Madame!' And she awarded me the proud look of a teacher whose pupil has showed unexpected intelligence. 'Monsieur Paul, after he has taken equal parts of goose breast and the finest pork, and broken a certain number of egg yolks into them, and ground them *very*, very fine, cooks all with seasoning for some three hours. *But*,' she pushed her face nearer, and looked with ferocious gloating at the *pâté* inside me, her eyes like X rays, 'he never stops stirring it! Figure to yourself the work of it – stir, stir, never stopping!

'Then he grinds in a suspicion of nutmeg, and then adds, very thoroughly, a glass of *marc* for each hundred grams of *pâté*. And is Madame not pleased?'

Again I agreed, rather timidly, that Madame was much pleased, that Madame had never, indeed, tasted such an

10

unctuous and exciting *pâté*. The girl wet her lips delicately, and then started as if she had been pin-stuck.

'But the trout! My God, the trout!' She grabbed the bucket, and her voice grew higher and more rushed.

'Here is the trout, Madame. You are to eat it *au bleu*, and you should never do so if you had not seen it alive. For if the trout were dead when it was plunged into the *court bouillon* it would not turn blue. So, naturally, it must be living.'

I knew all this, more or less, but I was fascinated by her absorption in the momentary problem. I felt quite ignorant, and asked her with sincerity, 'What about the trout? Do you take out its guts before or after?'

'Oh, the trout!' She sounded scornful. 'Any trout is glad, truly glad, to be prepared by Monsieur Paul. His little gills are pinched, with one flash of the knife he is empty, and then he curls in agony in the *bouillon* and all is over. And it is the curl you must judge, Madame. A false *truite au bleu* cannot curl.'

She panted triumph at me, and hurried out with the bucket.

III

She *is* a funny one, I thought, and for not more than two or three minutes I drank wine and mused over her. Then she darted in, with the trout correctly blue and agonizingly curled on a platter, and on her crooked arm a plate of tiny boiled potatoes and a bowl.

When I had been served and had cut off her anxious breathings with an assurance that the fish was the best I

11

had ever tasted, she peered again at me and at the sauce in the bowl. I obediently put some of it on the potatoes: no fool I, to ruin *truite au bleu* with a hot concoction! There was more silence.

'Ah!' she sighed at last. 'I knew Madame would feel thus! Is it not the most beautiful sauce in the world with the flesh of a trout?'

I nodded incredulous agreement.

'Would you like to know how it is done?'

I remembered all the legends of chefs who guarded favorite recipes with their very lives, and murmured yes.

She wore the exalted look of a believer describing a miracle at Lourdes as she told me, in a rush, how Monsieur Paul threw chopped chives into hot sweet butter and then poured the butter off, how he added another nut of butter and a tablespoonful of thick cream for each person, stirred the mixture for a few minutes over a slow fire, and then rushed it to the table.

'So simple?' I asked softly, watching her lighted eyes and the tender lustful lines of her strange mouth.

'So simple, Madame! But,' she shrugged, 'you know, with a master –'

I was relieved to see her go: such avid interest in my eating wore on me. I felt released when the door closed behind her, free for a minute or so from her victimization. What would she have done, I wondered, if I had been ignorant or unconscious of any fine flavors?

She was right, though, about Monsieur Paul. Only a master could live in this isolated mill and preserve his gastronomic dignity through loneliness and the sure financial loss of unused butter and addled eggs. Of

12

course there was the stream for his fish, and I knew his *pâtés* would grow even more edible with age; but how could he manage to have a thing like roasted lamb ready for any chance patron? Was the consuming interest of his one maid enough fuel for his flame?

I tasted the last sweet nugget of trout, the one nearest the blued tail, and poked somnolently at the minute white billiard balls that had been eyes. Fate could not harm me, I remembered winily, for I had indeed dined today, and dined well. Now for a leaf of crisp salad, and I'd be on my way.

The girl slid into the room. She asked me again, in a respectful but gossipy manner, how I had liked this and that and the other things, and then talked on as she mixed dressing for the endive.

'And now,' she announced, after I had eaten one green sprig and dutifully pronounced it excellent, 'now Madame is going to taste Monsieur Paul's special terrine, one that is not even on the summer menu, when a hundred covers are laid here daily and we have a headwaiter and a wine waiter, and cabinet ministers telegraph for tables! Madame will be pleased.'

And heedless of my low moans of the walk still before me, of my appreciation and my unhappily human and limited capacity, she cut a thick heady slice from the terrine of meat and stood over me while I ate it, telling me with almost hysterical pleasure of the wild ducks, the spices, the wines that went into it. Even surfeit could not make me deny that it was a rare dish. I ate it all, knowing my luck, and wishing only that I had red wine to drink with it.

13

I was beginning, though, to feel almost frightened, realizing myself an accidental victim of these stranded gourmets, Monsieur Paul and his handmaiden. I began to feel that they were using me for a safety valve, much as a thwarted woman relieves herself with tantrums or a fit of weeping. I was serving a purpose, and perhaps a noble one, but I resented it in a way approaching panic.

I protested only to myself when one of Monsieur Paul's special cheeses was cut for me, and ate it doggedly, like a slave. When the girl said that Monsieur Paul himself was preparing a special filter of coffee for me, I smiled servile acceptance: wine and the weight of food and my own character could not force me to argue with maniacs. When, before the coffee came, Monsieur Paul presented me, through his idolater, with the most beautiful apple tart I had ever seen, I allowed it to be cut and served to me. Not a wince or a murmur showed the waitress my distressed fearfulness. With a stuffed careful smile on my face, and a clear nightmare in my head of trussed wanderers prepared for his altar by this hermit-priest of gastronomy, I listened to the girl's passionate plea for fresh pastry dough.

'You cannot, you *can*not, Madame, serve old pastry!' She seemed ready to beat her breast as she leaned across the table. 'Look at that delicate crust! You may feel that you have eaten too much.' (I nodded idiotic agreement.) 'But this pastry is like feathers — it is like snow. It is in fact good for you, a digestive! And why?' She glared sternly at me. 'Because Monsieur Paul did not even open the flour bin until he saw you coming! He could not, he *could* not have baked you one of his special apple tarts with old dough!'

She laughed, tossing back her head and curling her mouth voluptuously.

IV

Somehow I managed to refuse a second slice, but I trembled under her surmise that I was ready for my special filter.

The wine and its fortitude had fled me, and I drank the hot coffee as a suffering man gulps ether, deeply and gratefully.

I remember, then, chatting with surprising glibness, and sending to Monsieur Paul flowery compliments, all of them sincere and well won, and I remember feeling only amusement when a vast glass of *marc* appeared before me and then gradually disappeared, like the light in the warm room full of water-sounds. I felt surprise to be alive still, and suddenly very grateful to the wild-lipped waitress, as if her presence had sustained me through duress. We discussed food and wine. I wondered bemusedly why I had been frightened.

The *marc* was gone. I went into the crowded bedroom for my jacket. She met me in the darkening hall when I came out, and I paid my bill, a large one. I started to thank her, but she took my hand, drew me into the dining room, and without words poured more spirits into my glass. I drank to Monsieur Paul while she watched me intently, her pale eyes bulging in the dimness and her lips pressed inward as if she too tasted the hot, aged *marc*.

The cat rose from his ferny bed, and walked contemptuously out of the room.

Suddenly the girl began to laugh, in a soft shy breathless way, and came close to me.

'Permit me!' she said, and I thought she was going to kiss me. But instead she pinned a tiny bunch of snowdrops and dark bruised cyclamens against my stiff jacket, very quickly and deftly, and then ran from the room with her head down.

I waited for a minute. No sounds came from anywhere in the old mill, but the endless rushing of the full stream seemed to strengthen, like the timed blare of an orchestra under a falling curtain.

She's a *funny* one, I thought. I touched the cool blossoms on my coat and went out, like a ghost from ruins, across the courtyard toward the dim road to Avallon.

Let the Sky Rain Potatoes

The Merry Wives of Windsor

There are two questions which can easily be asked about a potato: What is it, and Why is it?

Both these questions are irritating to a true amateur. The answers to the first are self-evident: a potato is a food, delicious, nourishing, and so on. The second question is perhaps too impertinent even to be answered, although many a weary housewife has felt like shouting it to the high heavens if her family has chanced to be the kind that takes for granted the daily appearance of this ubiquitous vegetable.

A dictionary will say that a potato is a farinaceous tuber used for food. An encyclopædia will cover eight or nine large pages with a sad analysis of its origins, modes of cultivation, and diseases, some of which are enough in themselves to discourage any potato enthusiast who might read them carefully.

Between these two extremes of definition is a story interesting even to one who is not overly fond of potatoes as a food. There are romance and colour, and the fine sound of brave names in its telling.

In Peru, the Spanish found *papas* growing in the early 1500s, and the monk Hieronymus Cardán took them back with him to his own people. The Italians liked them, and then the Belgians.

About that time, Sir Walter Raleigh found a potato in the American South, and carried it back to his estate near Cork. Some say it was a yam he had, thought strongly aphrodisiac by the Elizabethans. Some say it was a white potato. A German statue thanks Raleigh for bringing it to Europe. On the other hand, the Spanish claim recognition for its European introduction.

No matter what its origin, eat it, eat it, urged the British Royal Society. But for many decades its cultivation made but little progress.

By the time it had become important as a food, especially for poor people, its diseases also had matured, and in 1846 potato blight sent thousands of hungry Irishmen to their graves, or to America.

Warts and scabs and rusts and rots did their work, too, and men worked hard to breed new varieties of potatoes before newer plagues seized them. Great Scott, the Boston Comrade, Magnum Bonum, Rhoderick Dhu and Up-to-Date, Ninetyfold: these and many hundreds more filled pots around the world, and still do.

But no matter the name; a spud's a spud, and by any other name it would still be starchy, and covered with dusty cork for skin, and, what's worse, taken for granted on every blond-head's table.

If the men are darker, it is pastes in slender strings they'll eat, or tubes, always farinaceous, as the dictionary says; but more often on Anglo-Saxon fare the potato takes place before any foreign macaroni or spaghetti.

It is hard sometimes to say why. A potato is good when it is cooked correctly. Baked slowly, with its skin rubbed first in a buttery hand, or boiled in its jacket and then 'shook,' it is delicious. Salt and pepper are almost always necessary to its hot moist-dusty flavour. Alone, or with a fat jug of rich cool milk or a chunk of fresh Gruyère, it fills the stomach and the soul with a satisfaction not too easy to attain.

In general, however, a potato is a poor thing, poorly treated. More often than not it is cooked in so unthinking and ignorant a manner as to make one feel that it has never before been encountered in the kitchen, as when avocados were sent to the Cornish Mousehole by a lady who heard months later that their suave thick meat had been thrown away and the stones boiled and boiled to no avail.

'Never have I tasted such a poor, flaccid, grey sad mixture of a mess,' says my mother when she tells of the potatoes served in Ireland. And who would contradict her who has ever seen the baked-or-boiled in a London Lyons or an A.B.C.?

The Irish prefer them, evidently, to starvation, and the English, too. And in mid-western Europe, in a part where dumplings grow on every kitchen-range, there are great cannon balls of them, pernicious as any shrapnel to a foreign palate, but swallowed like feathery egg-whites by the natives.

They are served with goose at Christmas, and all around the year. They are the size of a toddling child's round head. They are grey, and exceedingly heavy. They are made painstakingly of grated raw potato, moulded, then boiled, then added to by moulding, then boiled again. Layer after layer is pressed on, cooked, and cooled, and finally the whole sodden pock-marked mass is bounced in bubbling goose broth until time to heave it to the platter.

Forks may bend against its iron-like curves, stomachs may curdle in a hundred gastric revolutions; a potato dumpling is more adamantine. It survives, and is served to ever-renewing decades of hungry yodelling mouths.

In itself, this always fresh desire for starch, for the potato, is important. No matter what its form, nor its national disguise, the appetite for it is there, impervious to the mandates of dictators or any other blight.

Perhaps its most insidious manifestation is that Anglo-Saxons take it for granted. A meal for them includes potatoes in some form; it always has, therefore it always will. And no revolt, no smouldering rebellion of the meal-planner, can change this smug acceptance.

Most important, however, is the potato's function as a gastronomic complement. It is this that should be considered, to rob it of its dangerous monotony, and clothe it with the changing mysterious garment of adaptability.

Although few realize it, to be complementary is in itself a compliment. It is a subtle pleasure, like the small exaltation of a beautiful dark woman who finds herself unexpectedly in the company of an equally beautiful blonde. It is what a great chef meant once when he repulsed a consolation.

He was a Frenchman, summoned to London when King Edward VII found that his subjects resented his dining more in Paris than at home.

This great cook one day prepared a dish of soles in such a manner that the guests at Edward's table waited assuredly for a kingly compliment. He was summoned. Their mouths hung open in sated expectation.

'The Château Yquem,' said Edward VII, 'was excellent.'

Later the master chef shrugged, a nonchalance denied by every muscle in his pleased face.

'How could my dish have had a greater compliment?' he demanded, calmly. 'His Majesty knows, as I do, that when a dish is perfect, as was my sole to-night, the wine is good. If the dish is lower than perfection, the wine, lacking its complement, tastes weak and poor. So – you see?'

Although there are few ways of preparing potatoes to make them approach the perfection of a royal plate of fish, and none I know of to make them worth the compliment of a bottle of Château Yquem, they in their own way are superlative complements. And it is thus, as I have said, that they should be treated.

If, French fried, they make a grilled sirloin of beef taste richer; if, mashed and whipped with fresh cream and salty butter, they bridge the deadly gap between a ragout and a salad; if, baked and pinched open and bulging with mealy snowiness, they offset the fat spiced flavour of a pile of sausages – then and then alone should they be served.

Then they are dignified. Then they are worthy of a high place, not debased to the deadly rank of daily acceptance. Then they are a gastronomic pleasure, not merely 'tubers used for food.'

How Not to Cook an Egg

Probably one of the most private things in the world is an egg until it is broken. Until then, you would think that its secrets are its own, hidden behind the impassive beautiful curvings of its shell, white or brown or speckled. It emerges full formed, almost painlessly, from the hen. It lies without thought in the straw, and unless there is a thunderstorm or a sharp rise in temperature, it stays fresh enough to please the human palate for several days.

In spite of the complete impersonality of its shell, however, some things about an egg can be guessed. Those who know how can decide several rather surprising facts about it by holding it before a strong light; and even a zany will tell you that if an egg is none too fresh, it will stand up and perhaps bob a little in a bowl of water. The best thing to do with aged eggs is not to buy them, since they are fit for nothing, and a poor economy.

Hens, as long as they can find enough to eat, go right along at their chosen profession whether the country is at war or not; but unfortunately the product of their industry is so delicate and so perishable that when most of the fast trucks and trains of the land are being used to shift soldiers here and there, the price of eggs goes much too high for comfort, whether or not the supply is ample.

During the last war housewives used to buy several dozen eggs when the price was down, and cover them in a crock with a singularly unpleasant stuff called water glass. I can remember going to the cellar and fishing around in a stone jar for two eggs for a cake; the jellied chemical made a sucking noise as I spooned out the thickly coated, hideous stuff, and I felt squeamish and afraid. I decided then – and I still hold to it – that I would rather eat a good fresh egg only occasionally than have a whole cellarful of the dishonest old ones that can be used only in cakes and cookies.

The finest way, of course, to know that your egg is fresh is to own the hen that makes it. This scheme has many drawbacks; and I for one, as a person who has never felt any bond of sympathy between myself and chickens (their heads are too small, somehow, for their stupid, scratching, omnivorous bodies), have always been content to let someone else tend to the hen house, even if I had to pay much more for the product.

Eggs are a good investment now and then, expensive or not; and unless you are told otherwise by your doctor, or hate them in any form, they should be eaten in place of meat occasionally. The old-fashioned idea that they are 'invalid food,' something light and inconsequential, is fairly well proved foolish by the fact that two eggs are fully as nutritious as a juicy beefsteak – but ten times as hard to digest unless they are cooked with great wisdom.

Probably the wisest way to treat an egg is not to cook it at all. An accomplished barfly will prove to you that a Prairie Oyster is one of the quickest pickups known to man; and whether you are hung over, or merely tired, a raw egg beaten with a little milk or Sherry can shortly make you feel much more able to cope with yourself.

A biochemist once told me that every minute an egg is cooked makes it take three hours longer to digest. The thought of a stomach pumping and grinding and laboring for some nine hours over an average three-minute egg is wearisome, if true, and makes memories of picnics and deviled eggs seem haunting.

The simplest way to eat an egg, if you refuse to swallow it raw, even in its fanciest high-tasting disguises, is to boil it. Rather it is *not* to boil it, for no more erroneous phrase ever existed than 'to boil an egg.'

There are several ways not to 'boil' an egg so that it will be tender, thoroughly cooked, and yet almost as easily digested as if it were raw.

One fairly good one is to drop the egg gently into simmering water, first running cold water over it so that it will not crack, and then let it stand there in the gentle heat for whatever time you wish. It will cook just as fast as if the water were hopping about in great bubbles, and it will be a better treated egg.

The best way, I think, is to cover the egg with cold water in a little pan. Heat briskly, and as soon as the water begins to bubble, the egg is done. It will be more tender than when started in hot water, which, of course, makes the part nearest the shell cook immediately, instead of heating the whole thing gently.

I have never yet seen an egg crack when started in cool water; but some people automatically make a pinhole in every egg they boil, to prevent possible leaks and lesions, and their inevitable losses.

If you still want hard-boiled eggs, after pondering the number of days it would take to digest them, start them in cold water, turn off the heat as soon as the water begins to bubble, and let the eggs stand until cold. They will be tender, and comparatively free from nightmares.

If you think eggs boiled in their shells are fit food for the nursery, and refuse to admit any potential blessing in one delicately prepared, neatly spooned from its shell into a cup, sagely seasoned with salt and fresh-ground black pepper and a sizeable dollop of butter, all to be eaten with hot toast, then egg in the shell is definitely not your dish. Try heating, instead, a shallow skillet, skirling a lump of butter or bacon grease in it until it looks very hot, and breaking a fresh egg or two into it. Then – and this is the trick – turn off the heat at once, cover the pan tightly, and wait for about three minutes. The result will be tender and firm, and very good, indeed, with toast and coffee, or with a salad and white wine for supper.

This method, of course, is a compromise. It is not a fried egg, strictly speaking; yet it is as near to making a good fried egg as I have ever got.

I can make amazingly bad fried eggs; and in spite of what people tell me, I continue to make amazingly bad fried eggs – tough, and with edges like some kind of dirty starched lace, and a taste part sulphur and part singed newspaper. The best way to find a trustworthy method, I think, is to ask almost anyone but me. Or look in a cook book. Or experiment.

There are as many different theories about making an omelette as there are people who like them; but heading the list are two main schools: the French, which uses eggs hardly stirred together, and the puffy, or soufflé, which beats the white and the yellow parts of the eggs separately, and then mixes them. Then, of course, there is the Italian *frittata* school, which stirs in all kinds of cooked, cooled vegetables with eggs, and merges them into a sort of pie. And a very good school that is.

Moreover, there is the Oriental school, best exemplified by what is usually called *foo yeung* in chop-suey parlors, which is a kind of pancake of egg and bean sprouts and *ad infinitum*.

To cap the whole thing, there is the school which has its own dependable and usually very simple method of putting eggs in a pan and having them come out as intended. Brillat-Savarin called them *oeufs brouillis*, but I call them simply 'scrambled eggs.'

The best definition of a perfect French omelette is given, perhaps unwittingly, in the American translation of Escoffier's *Guide Culinaire*: 'scrambled eggs enclosed in a coating of coagulated egg.' This phrase in itself is none too appetizing, but it must do for want of a better, though no such disparagement can be attached to the omelette.

Basic French Omelette. In a smooth 8-or 10-inch frying pan heat 3 tablespoons butter until it gives off a nutty smell, but does not brown. ('This will not only lend an exquisite taste,' Escoffier says, 'but the degree of heat reached in order to produce the aroma will be found to insure the perfect setting of the eggs.' Roll the pan to cover the sides with butter.

Beat 6 eggs lightly with a fork, add seasoning, and pour into the pan. As soon as the edges are set, slide a spatula under the center so that all the uncooked part will run under the cooked. Repeat this operation once or twice, never leaving the omelette to its own devices. When it is daintily browned on the bottom and creamy on the top, fold it in the middle (or roll it, if you are a master), slide it on to a dish, and serve without more ado.

Chopped herbs, cheese, mushrooms, and almost anything else may be added at your discretion, either in the stirred eggs, or at the moment that the omelette is ready to fold.

The second school of omelettes is roughly defined as belonging to those addicts who believe eggs should be separated, beaten hard, and then brought together again. Probably the main trick to remember in this technique is that the resulting foamy delicate mass should be cooked slowly instead of fast. If such is done, 'it will stand up firm and proud, instead of collapsing like a tired horse,' says Mrs. Mazzi.

Basic Soufflé Omelette. Separate 6 eggs, and beat the whites until they are very stiff, and the yolks until they are creamy. Add seasoning, and 5 tablespoons hot water to the yolks, mix well, and fold in the whites.

Heat a smooth skillet, add the butter, and roll it around the sides until it bubbles. Pour in the egg mixture, and leave the skillet over a very low fire until the omelette is brown on the bottom. Place it under a broiler to brown lightly on top. Test, as for a cake, with a toothpick, which should come out dry and clean when the omelette is cooked.

This omelette can be cut in two parts, and filled or sauced with chicken livers, Spanish sauce, left-over creamed sweet-breads, mushrooms in Sherry, and so on.

Or try sprinkling it with powdered sugar, pouring a little rum over it, and flaming it for a fine dessert. Or spread it with chutney or any good preserve, and grill it again very quickly for a strange, savory tailpiece to a meal.

An Italian *frittata*, which like all omelettes is a fine dish for lunch or supper in any language, is a kind of pie or pancake filled with vegetables. It is made, if possible, with olive oil instead of butter. Whatever odorous mulch of herbs and legumes that you decide to make should be cooled and then added to the eggs, though it would be well to start with a fairly sound example.

Frittata of courgette. Heat 3 tablespoons olive oil in a skillet, and cook in it for 10 minutes 1 onion, or 3 small green onions, and a clove of garlic, all finely minced. Add 5 small courgette cut into thin slices, 1 large fresh tomato, peeled and cut up, or 1 cup solid-pack canned tomatoes, salt and pepper, and 1 teaspoon herbs – parsley, sweet marjoram, or thyme. Cover, and cook until the vegetable is tender. Take from the stove and cool. Beat 9 eggs lightly, season them, and mix with cooled vegetables. Pour the whole back into the skillet, cover the pan tightly, and cook over a slow fire until the edges of the *frittata* pull away from the pan. If the middle puffs up, prick it with a long sharp knife.

When the omelette is solid, brown it lightly under a slow broiler flame in a pre-heated oven, cut in slices like a pie, and serve at once.

This *frittata* can be made with almost anything – string beans, peas, spinach, artichokes. Cheese can be sprinkled over it. Different kinds of herbs, like sweet basil, summer savory, and on and on, can change its whole character. And with a glass of wine and some honest-to-God bread, it is a meal.

Foo Yeung is really another cut off the same loaf. The main difference is that in the Oriental version the vegetables are sliced and cooked only until they are crisply heated, so that the whole texture is one of surprises, a mixture of sharp and soft, crisp and mellow, as all good Chinese dishes should be. This recipe can, of course, use gourmet powder (*mei jing*), diced roasted pork (*for juk*), diced peeled water chestnuts (*ma tai*), diced bamboo shoots (*jook tsun*), and a dozen other delicious things which are sold in Chinese stores. It can also be made without any of them, and still taste as fresh and strange as any genuine Chinese omelette.

Basic Foo Yeung. Brown lightly ½ cup chopped onion in 3 tablespoons good fat. Stir into the eggs the following chopped vegetables: ½ cup celery, ½ cup green pepper, ½ cup mushrooms. Let the eggs become firm and brown in the pan, stirring up the center once in a while. Cut the omelette into sections, and serve quickly.

There are almost as many variations to this recipe as there are Chinese characters. Add shrimps. Add cooked rice. Add diced chicken. Add fried almonds. Try mixing all the ingredients together and then frying in little cakes in the hot fat. Your method depends on whether you come from Canton, Chungsja, or West Hollywood.

Almost every good cook in the world has at least one egg ritual, usually histrionic – and more power to him! Here are three, fully guaranteed (although one of them is far from economical, and is recommended only for those occasions known as state).

Eggs in Hell. Heat 4 tablespoons olive oil in a saucepan with a tight cover. Split a clove of garlic lengthwise, run a toothpick through each half, and brown the halves slowly in the oil. Add an onion, minced, and cook it until it is golden. Then add 2 cups tomato sauce (the Italian kind is best, but even catsup will do if you cut down on other spices). Then add 1 teaspoon mixed minced herbs, such as basil and thyme, and 1 teaspoon minced parsley, and salt and pepper to taste. Cook for about 15 minutes, stirring often, and then remove the garlic. Into this sauce break 6 eggs. Spoon the sauce over them, cover the pan closely, and cook very slowly until the eggs are done, or for about 15 minutes. (If the skillet is a heavy one, you can turn off the flame and cook the eggs 15 minutes with the heat stored in the metal.) When the eggs are done, put them carefully on slices of thin, dry, toasted French bread, and cover them with sauce. Grated Parmesan or a similar cheese is good on this dish.

One of the many variations of this recipe that we used to make, never earlier than 2:00 and never later than 4:00 in the morning, was in a strange, modernistic electric kitchen on the wine-terraces between Lausanne and Montreux. We put cream and Worcestershire sauce into little casseroles, and heated them into a bubble. Then we broke eggs into them, turned off the current, and waited until they looked done, while we stood around drinking Champagne with circles under our eyes, and Viennese music in our heads. We ate the eggs with spoons and went to bed.

A fair substitute for those far-away delightful shadows

is the invention of a young painter in Mexico. This recipe, like most good ones, has many variations; but unlike most of them, it is inexpensive. It leads, by a somewhat crooked path, to what I think is the best way to cook eggs (unless you count hard-boiling them, cracking them on your own head, and eating them with salt and pepper and a glass of cold beer some hot Summer day).

Eggs Obstaculos. Heat in a shallow dish 2 tablespoons butter or olive oil with ¾ cup hot tomato sauce, or ¾ cup tomato sauce seasoned with 8 drops Tabasco, rolling the mixture well around the edges. When the sauce bubbles, break 8 eggs into it. Heat slowly until the eggs are done, pour 1 cup beer over them, and serve at once with hot toast.

Scrambled eggs have been made – and massacred – for as long as people have known about pots and pans. Very few now know the rudiments held in this recipe. I have tried it at least a hundred times, on people as various as a three-year-old Irishman and a poet-laureate. I have also tried to tell four cooks how to make it. Three of them were professionals, and one was willing to learn. All failed.

Scrambled Eggs. Break 8 good fresh eggs gently into a cold iron skillet. Pour ½ pint rich cream in, and stir quietly until the whole is blended, but not longer. Never beat or whip. Heat very slowly, stirring from the middle bottom in large curds, as seldom as possible. Never let the mixture bubble. Add seasoning of salt and freshly ground pepper at the last stir or two. The stirring takes perhaps a half-hour. It cannot be hurried. Serve on toast, when the mixture is barely firm. Herbs or cheese or mushrooms, or chicken livers and the like may be added for embellishment when the eggs are half done.

It is a poor figure of a man who will say that eggs are fit only to be eaten at breakfast, served as they can be in these and countless other fashions. Let him ponder these methods, and if, wisely or not, he should choose from all the possible forms an egg fresh-broken from the shell, cupped with a bit of lemon juice and pepper and any other seasoning to hand, and called an Oyster, we can but hope that he has drunk well the night before, and slept the sleep of the satisfied – if not of the just.

Love was the Pearl

Then love was the pearl of his oyster,
And Venus rose red out of wine.

– Dolores, C. A. Swinburne

The love-life of an oyster is a curious one, dependent on the vagaries of temperature and the tides. If its world is warm, if the water around it is about seventy degrees, it is able to send out a little potent flood of milt and thus excite a female to her monstrous spawning, now five million eggs, now fifty. And if the tide is right, the milt will meet the eggs, and spats will result.

Spatting and spawning, spawning and spatting . . .

The love-life of a man has also been called curious, and part of it has long depended on the mysterious powers of this bi-valved mollusc which most of the dictionaries say is usually eaten alive.

Women have been known to be influenced, and whether to the good or nay is not for me to say, by the schemed use of these shellfish, and there is one man named Mussolini who lives near Biloxi, in Mississippi, who swears that he has cured seven frigid virgins by the judicious feeding of long brownish buck-oysters from near-by bayous.

It is men, though, in astounding numbers, who will swear, in correctly modulated voices, a hundred equally strange facts. Women of the East, they will tell you if you are acceptable for such confessions, are built crossways, so that love-making is even more exotic than erotic with them. They know it for a fact. And there is an equally astounding number of men, and some of them have actually graduated from Yale, and even Princeton, who know positively that oysters are an aphrodisiac . . . one of the best. They can tell of countless chaps whose powers have been increased nigh unto the billy-goat's, simply from eating raw cold oysters.

There are many reasons why an oyster is supposed to have this desirable quality, embarrassing if true . . . and although the term is literally incorrect, most of them are old wives' tales.

Most of them are physiological, too, and have to do with an oyster's odor, its consistency, and probably its strangeness. All of them, apparently, are fond but false hopes, and no more to be relied on than that a horse-hair dropped into a trough in the full of the moon will swim about and hiss, an honest-to-God snake.

There was a thin little man once, at Harvard probably. He was not quite a virgin, being about twenty-two years old, and for some reason he managed to date himself, one wintry Saturday night, with a very very terrible very very divine girl of the upper classes known by young men of the same classes as La Belle Dame sans Culottes.

The thin little man, hardly more than a lad as his Grandfather used to say, felt full of tremblings and awed withdrawals, and consulted with several of his more obviously virile friends. Oysters, they said firmly. Oysters are the answer.

So about noon on the dated Saturday the chapkin dropped in at the Grand Central Oyster Bar. It was December, and the oysters, raw and chilled, were not only delicious but correctly in season for any and all correct young men. Ours bolstered himself with some ale, all by himself but still thinking of it (since English B4 with good old pipe-smoking Cyril Dinwiddie) as a noggin rather than a glass, and ate one dozen more than he really wanted.

About two o'clock he was horrified to see that it was not three, and roamed thinly into the cold streets, his mind trying with a dawning hopelessness to call up some of the more torrid reminiscences of his approaching date . . . reminiscences of his roommates, that is.

He took a taxi to the Plaza Grill, looked with what jauntiness he could summon at the raddled brokers eating delicious things like scrambled eggs and hot baked potatoes, and ordered another dozen oysters. He wished it was about six o'clock . . . by then there would at least be one or two lovely actresses to peek at, and he would be within an hour of . . . of . . .

He ordered another dozen.

A little later he walked over to Sixth Avenue and headed boggily toward the RKO Gateway. He had always liked oyster-bars. He had always thought they were fun, removed as they were for the most part from the shrill chitterings of debutantes. But now, as it grew dark and people scuttled for busses all about him, he began to think that a sweet little debutante sipping her tea-and-Martinis at '21' would be heaven. He could pay the bill when she was finished with her childlike pleasures, take her to her mother's safely respectable elevator . . . and go home.

But tonight he was meeting the Belle of the Balls . . . and alone . . .

He turned into the Gateway, and in a small hopeless voice ordered two dozen blue points.

When the bar-man peered at him he snapped, in a masculine way he hoped, 'That's what I said, isn't it?' For a minute he felt almost warmed by his own unsuspected fire, and then as he started diligently to swallow his prescription he was nearly overcome by a dreadful weariness, so that if he had not represented the Alma Mater he surmised he did, he would have stretched out quietly on the soft-looking white tile floor and given himself to safe dreams.

Instead, he pulled in his stomach as far as he could, and sipped seemingly at his ale, and gradually ate two dozen more of the same.

About six-thirty that night, this thin little man, looking much older than twenty-two for the first time in his life, walked slowly and uncertainly up the steps of the Harvard or whatever Club. Visions of rosy flesh and honey-colored thighs were quite wiped out, at last, by the chill certainty that Old Chick and Old Bill and Old Rot-Gut had betrayed him. Yes, he was betrayed . . . thank God.

Bed, he thought solemnly. Bed is what I need . . . and *alone*. I'm still a man, he thought with his last remaining spark of masculinity . . . I'm still a man, in *spite* of the blasted shell-fish . . .

And he stuck out his chest and almost fell flat on his peaked oyster-colored face.

'Here, *here*, sir,' the porter clucked, feeling some-what wearily that another chance to prove himself a real father stared him in the face. 'Not *here*, sir. You just come with me.'

And he tucked his arm winningly, seductively, with practiced skill, into the thin little man's, and together they wove toward a comfortable couch.

G is for Gluttony

. . . And why and how it is that.

It is a curious fact that no man likes to call himself a glutton, and yet each of us has in him a trace of gluttony, potential or actual. I cannot believe that there exists a single coherent human being who will not confess, at least to himself, that once or twice he has stuffed himself to the bursting point, on anything from quail financière to flapjacks, for no other reason than the beastlike satisfaction of his belly. In fact I pity anyone who has not permitted himself this sensual experience, if only to determine what his own private limitations are, and where, for himself alone, gourmandism ends and gluttony begins.

It is different for each of us, and the size of a man's paunch has little to do with the kind of appetite which fills it. Diamond Jim Brady, for instance, is more often than not called 'the greatest glutton in American history,' and so on, simply because he had a really enormous capacity for food. To my mind he was not gluttonous but rather monstrous, in that his stomach was about six times normal size. That he ate at least six times as much as a normal man did not make him a glutton. He was, instead, Gargantuan, in the classical sense. His taste was keen and sure to the time of his death, and that he ate nine portions of sole Marguéry the night George Rector brought the recipe back to New York from Paris especially for him does not mean that he gorged himself upon it but simply that he had room for it.

I myself would like to be able to eat that much of something I really delight in, and I can recognize overtones of envy in the way lesser mortals so easily damned Brady as a glutton, even in the days of excess when he flourished.

Probably this country will never again see so many fat, rich men as were prevalent at the end of the last century, copper kings and railroad millionaires and suchlike literally stuffing themselves to death in imitation of Diamond Jim, whose abnormally large stomach coincided so miraculously with the period. He ate a hundred men like 'Betcha-Million' Gates into their oversized coffins simply because he was a historical accident, and it is interesting to speculate on what his influence would be today, when most of the robber barons have gastric ulcers and lunch off crackers and milk at their desks. Certainly it is now unfashionable to overeat in public, and the few real trenchermen left are careful to practice their gastronomical excesses in the name of various honorable and respected food-and-wine societies.

It is safe to say, I think, that never again in our civilization will gluttony be condoned, much less socially accepted, as it was at the height of Roman decadence, when a vomitorium was as necessary a part of any well-appointed home as a powder room is today, and throat-ticklers were as common as our Kleenex. That was, as one almost forgotten writer has said in an unforgettable phrase, the 'period of insatiable voracity and the peacock's plume,' and I am glad it is far behind me, for I would make but a weak social figure of a glutton, no matter to what excesses of hunger I could confess.

My capacity is very limited, fortunately for my inward as well as outer economy, so that what gluttonizing I have indulged in has resulted in biliousness more spiritual than physical. It has, like almost everyone's in this century, been largely secret. I think it reached its peak of purely animal satisfaction when I was about seventeen.

I was cloistered then in a school where each avid, yearning young female was allowed to feed at least one of her several kinds of hunger with a daily chocolate bar. I evolved for myself a strangely voluptuous pattern of borrowing, hoarding, begging, and otherwise collecting about seven or eight of these noxious sweets and eating them alone upon a pile of pillows when all the other girls were on the hockey field or some such equally healthful place. If I could eat at the same time a nickel box of soda crackers, brought to me by a stooge among the day girls, my orgiastic pleasure was complete.

I find, in confessing this far-distant sensuality, that even the cool detachment acquired with time does not keep me from feeling both embarrassed and disgusted. What a pig I was!

I am a poor figure of a glutton today in comparison with that frank adolescent cramming. In fact I can think of nothing quite like it in my present make-up. It is true that I overeat at times, through carelessness or a deliberate prolonging of my pleasure in a certain taste, but I do not do it with the voracity of youth. I am probably incapable, really, of such lust. I rather regret it: one more admission of my dwindling powers!

Perhaps the nearest I come to gluttony is with wine. As often as possible, when a really beautiful bottle is before me, I drink all I can of it, even when I know that I have had more than I want physically. That is gluttonous.

But I think to myself, when again will I have this taste upon my tongue? Where else in the world is there just such wine as this, with just this bouquet, at just this heat, in just this crystal cup? And when again will I be alive to it as I am this very minute, sitting here on a green hillside above the sea, or here in this dim, murmuring, richly odorous restaurant, or here in this fishermen's café on the wharf? More, more, I think – all of it, to the last exquisite drop, for there is no satiety for me, nor ever has been, in such drinking.

Perhaps this keeps it from being gluttony – not according to the dictionary but in my own lexicon of taste. I do not know.

1

The word *financière*, for fairly obvious reasons, means richness, extravagance, a nonchalant disregard of the purse, but I sometimes suspect that I use it oftener than it warrants to denote anything Lucullan. I need only reread some Victorian cookery books to reassure myself and justify my preoccupation with the word.

I imagine that now and then, in the remotest dining clubs of London and Lisbon, in the most desperately spendthrift of *nouveaux-riches* private kitchens, quails are still served à *la financière*, and unless I am much mistaken they are prepared almost to the letter as Queen Victoria's kitchen contemporaries did them. Her own chef Francatelli scamps on the sauce but elaborates with pardonable smugness his method for the whole entrée, and his rival Soyer of the Reform Club makes up for it by giving a recipe for the sauce alone that would stun modern gourmets.

Herewith I present them both, *chefs-d'oeuvres* of two dashing culinary kings, flashing-eyed, soft-lipped prancing fellows if the engravings printed at their own expense in their two cookbooks are even half true.

SOYER'S SAUCE À LA FINANCIÈRE

Put a wineglassful of sherry into a stewpan with a piece of glaze the size of a walnut, and a bay-leaf, place it upon the fire, and when it boils add a quart of demi-glace; let it boil ten minutes, keeping it stirred; then add twelve fresh blanched mushrooms, twelve prepared cock's-combs, a throat sweetbread cut in thin slices, two French preserved truffles also in slices, and twelve small veal forcemeat quenelles; boil altogether ten minutes, skim it well, thin it with a little consommé if desired, but it must be rather thick, and seasoned very palatably.

This is of course from *The Gastronomic Regenerator*, which the famous Reform Club's even more famous chef dedicated to the Duke of Cambridge in 1847. It can be assumed at our safe distance that the Queen's cook needed no lessons from the Club's, but even so Francatelli's sauce recipe is less interesting. His detailed method, though, for preparing the quail with and for the sauce is a fine prose poem to the God of Gastronomical Surfeit, and I give it here for modern pondering.

FRANCATELLI'S QUAILS À LA FINANCIÈRE

Remove the bones entirely from eight fat quails, reserve the livers, and add to them half a pound of fat livers of fowl, with which prepare some force-meat, and stuff the quails with part of this; they must then be trussed in the usual manner, and placed in a stewpan with layers of fat bacon under them, a garnished faggot of parsley in the centre, and covered with layers of fat bacon; moisten with some wine mirepoix, *and braize them gently for about three-quarters of an hour. Prepare a rich* Financière *sauce, which must be finished with some of the liquor in which the quails have been braized. When about to send to table, warm the quails, drain and dish them up, garnish the centre with the* Financière, *pour some of the sauce around the entrée, and serve.*

This recipe is rather reminiscent of Brillat-Savarin's method for pheasant à la Sainte Alliance, although less pure, gastronomically speaking. He would, I think, have shuddered at applying it in no matter how simplified a form to quails, of which he wrote, 'A man betrays his ignorance every time he serves one cooked otherwise than roasted or *en papillote*, for its aroma is most fragile, and dissolves, evaporates, and vanishes whenever the little creature comes in contact with a liquid.'

It has always astonished and horrified me that this pretty wild bird, which Brillat-Savarin called 'the daintiest and most charming' of all of them, should be so thoroughly unpleasant to clean, once killed. Its innards, supposedly nourished on the tenderest of herbs and grains, send out a stench that is almost insupportable, and hunters dread the moment when they must cope with it, in order to savor somewhat later one of the finest tastes in all the world.

The best of these that I have ever eaten were in Juárez, Mexico, in two shoddy, delightful 'clubs' where illegal game was cooked by Chinese chefs, the quails grilled quickly over desert-bush coals, split open flat, and brought sizzling and charred to the table, innocent of grease or seasoning, and served with a dollop of strangely agreeable cactus-apple conserve. They were superb, thus unhampered.

A recipe I would follow if I could is the classical one for Quails in Ashes, *Cailles sous la Cendre*, a true hunters' rule, whose prime requisite is a fine log fire!

Each clean, emptied bird is wrapped in thickly buttered grape leaves and good bacon. (This is supposedly late summer, when the grain-fattened birds have fled before the guns to the high fertile meadows, just before the vineyards begin to turn gold.) Then they are enclosed in sturdy, buttered 'parchment' paper, put in the hot ashes, and left there for a half hour or a little more, with fresher hotter cinders raked over them from time to time. When ready to be served, the paper is cut off, and the inward-reaching layers of bacon, grape leaf, and tender quail send out such a vapor, I know, as would rouse Lazarus.

Once a Tramp, Always . . .

There is a mistaken idea, ancient but still with us, that an overdose of anything from fornication to hot chocolate will teach restraint by the very results of its abuse. A righteous and worried father, feeling broadminded and full of manly understanding, will urge a rich cigar upon his fledgling and almost force him to be sick, to show him how to smoke properly. Another, learning that his sons have been nipping dago red, will chain them psychologically to the dinner table and drink them under it, to teach them how to handle their liquor like gentlemen. Such methods are drastic and of dubious worth, I think. People continue to smoke and to drink, and to be excessive or moderate according to their own needs. Their good manners are a matter more of innate taste than of outward training.

Craving – the actual and continued need for something – is another matter. Sometimes it lasts for one's lifetime. There is no satisfying it, except temporarily, and that can spell death or ruin. At least three people I know very well, children of alcoholic parents, were literally born drunk, and after sad experience they face the hideous fact that one more nip will destroy them. But they dream of it. Another of my friends dreams of chocolate, and is haunted by sensory fantasies of the taste and smell of chocolate, and occasionally talks of chocolate the way some people talk of their mistresses, but one Hershey bar would damn him and his liver, too. (Members of A.A. pray to God daily to keep them from taking that First Drink. A first candy bar can be as dangerous.) These people choose to live, no matter how cautiously, because they know that they can never be satisfied. For them real satiety, the inner spiritual kind, is impossible. They are, although in a noble way, cheating: an *honest* Satur will risk death from exhaustion, still happily aware that there will always be more women in the world than he can possibly accommodate.

Somewhere between the extremes of putative training in self-control and unflagging discipline against wild cravings lie the sensual and voluptuous gastronomical favorites-of-a-lifetime, the nostalgic yearnings for flavors once met in early days – the smell or taste of a gooseberry pie on a summer noon at Peachblow Farm, the whiff of anise from a Marseille bar. Old or moderately young, of any sex, most of us can forgo the analyst's couch at will and call up some such flavors. It is better thus. Kept verbal, there is small danger of indigestion, and, in truth, a gooseberry pie can be a horror (those pale beady acid fruits, the sugar never masking their mean acidity, the crust sogging . . . my father rhapsodized occasionally about the ones at Peachblow and we tried to recapture their magic for him, but it was impossible). And a glass of *pastis* at the wrong time and with the wrong people can turn into a first-class emetic, no matter how it used to make the mind and body rejoice in Provence. Most people like to talk, once steered onto the right track, about their lifetime favorites in food. It does not matter if they have only dreamed of them for the past countless decades: favorites remain, and man-kind is basically a faithful bunch of fellows. If you loved Gaby Deslys or Fanny Brice, from no matter how far afar, you still can and do. And why not? There is, in this happily insatiable fantasizing, no saturation point, no moment at which the body must cry *Help!*

Of course, the average person has not actually pos-sessed a famous beauty, and it is there that gastronomy serves as a kind of surrogate, to ease our longings. One does not need to be a king or mogul to indulge most, if not all, of his senses with the heady enjoyment of a dish – speaking in culinary terms, that is. I myself, to come right down to it, have never been in love from afar, except perhaps for a handful of fleeting moments when a flickering shot of Wallace Reid driving over a cliff would make me feel queer. I know of women who have really mooned, and for years, over some such glamorous shadow, and it is highly possible that my own immunity is due to my sensual satisfaction, even vicarious, in such things as potato chips and Beluga caviar. This realization is cruelly matter-of-fact to anyone of romantic sensitiv-ity, and I feel vaguely apologetic about it. At the same time, I am relieved. I know that even though I eat potato chips perhaps once every three years, I can, whenever I wish to, tap an almost unlimited fountain of them not five hundred feet from my own door. It is not quite the same thing with caviar, of course, and I have smiled upon a one-pound tin of it, fresh and pearly gray, not more than eight or nine times in my life. But I know that for a time longer the acipensers of the Black and Caspian Seas will be able to carry out their fertility rites and that

I may even partake again of their delectable fruits. Meanwhile, stern about potato chips on the one hand and optimistic about Beluga on the other, I can savor with my mind's palate their strange familiarity.

It is said that a few connoisseurs, such as old George Saintsbury, can recall *physically* the bouquet of certain great vintages a half century after tasting them. I am a mouse among elephants now, but I can say just as surely that this minute, in a northern-California valley, I can taste-smell-hear-see and then feel between my teeth the potato chips I ate slowly one November afternoon in 1936, in the bar of the Lausanne Palace. They were uneven in both thickness and color, probably made by a new apprentice in the hotel kitchen, and almost surely they smelled faintly of either chicken or fish, for that was always the case there. They were a little too salty, to encourage me to drink. They were ineffable. I am still nourished by them. That is probably why I can be so firm about not eating my way through barrels, tunnels, mountains more of them here in the land where they hang like square cellophane fruit on wire trees in all the grocery stores, to tempt me sharply every time I pass them.

As for the caviar, I can wait. I know I cannot possibly, *ever*, eat enough of it to satisfy my hunger, my unreasonable lust, so I think back with what is almost placidity upon the times I could dig into a tub of it and take five minutes or so for every small voluptuous mouthful. Again, why not? Being carnal, such dreams are perforce sinful in some vocabularies. Other ways of thinking might call them merely foolish, or Freudian 'substitutes.' That is all right; I know that I can cultivate restraint, or

accept it patiently when it is thrust upon me – just as I
know that I can walk right down Main Street this minute
and buy almost as many Macadamia nuts as I would like
to eat, and certainly enough to make me feel very sick
for a time, but that I shan't do so.

I have some of the same twinges of basic craving for
those salty gnarled little nuts from Hawaii as the ones I
keep ruthlessly at bay for the vulgar fried potatoes and
the costly fish eggs. Just writing of my small steady passion for them makes my mouth water in a reassuringly
controlled way, and I am glad there are dozens of jars of
them in the local goodies shoppe, for me not to buy. I
cannot remember when I first ate a Macadamia, but I
was hooked from that moment. I think it was about
thirty years ago. The Prince of Wales was said to have
invested in a ranch in Hawaii which raised them in small
quantities, so that the name stuck in my mind because
he did, but I doubt that royal business cunning had
much to do with my immediate delectation. The last
time I ate one was about four months ago, in New York.
I surprised my *belle-secur* and almost embarrassed myself
by letting a small moan escape me when she put a bowl
of them beside my chair; they were beautiful – so lumpy,
Macadamian, salty, golden! And I ate one, to save face.
Oh, I can still sense its peculiar crispness and its complete Macadamianimity. How fortunate I am!

Many of the things we batten on in our fantasies are
part of our childhoods, although none of mine have
been, so far in this list. I was perhaps twenty-three when
I first ate almost enough caviar – not to mention any
caviar at all that I can now remember. It was one of the

best, brightest days of my whole life with my parents, and lunching in the quiet back room at the Café de la Paix was only a part of the luminous whole. My mother ate fresh foie gras, sternly forbidden to her liver, but she loved the cathedral at Strasbourg enough to risk almost any kind of attack, and this truffled slab was so plainly the best of her lifetime that we all agreed it could do her nothing but good, which it did. My father and I ate caviar, probably Sevruga, with green-black smallish beads and a superb challenge of flavor for the iced grassy vodka we used to cleanse our happy palates. We ate three portions apiece, tacitly knowing it could never happen again that anything would be quite so mysteriously perfect in both time and space. The headwaiter sensed all this, which is, of course, why he was world-known, and the portions got larger, and at our third blissful command he simply put the tin in its ice bowl upon our table. It was a regal gesture, like being tapped on the shoulder with a sword. We bowed, served ourselves exactly as he would have done, grain for grain, and had no need for any more. It was reward enough to sit in the almost empty room, chaste rococo in the slanting June sunlight, with the generous tub of pure delight between us, Mother purring there, the vodka seeping slyly through our veins, and real wood strawberries to come, to make us feel like children again and not near-gods. That was a fine introduction to what I hope is a reasonably long life of such occasional bliss.

As for potato chips, I do not remember them earlier than my twenty-first year, when I once ate stupidly and well of them in a small, stylish restaurant in Germany, where we had to wait downstairs in the tavern while our meal was being readied to eat upstairs. Beside me on a table was a bowl of exquisitely fresh and delicate chips, and when we finally sat down I could not face the heavily excellent dinner we had ordered. I was ashamed of my gluttony, for it is never commendable, even when based on ignorance. Perhaps *that* is why I am so stern today about not eating any of the devilish temptations?

There is one other thing I know I shall never get enough of – champagne. I cannot say when I drank my first prickly, delicious glass of it. I was raised in Prohibition, which meant that my father was very careful about his bootleggers, but the general adult drinking stayed around pinch-bottle Scotch as safest in those days, and I think I probably started my lifelong affair with Dom Pérignon's discovery in 1929, when I first went to France. It does not matter. I would gladly ask for the end of even a poor peasant there, who is given a glass of champagne on his deathbed to cheer him on his way.

I used to think, in my Russian-novel days, that I would cherish a lover who managed through thick and thin, snow and sleet, to have a bunch of Parma violets on my breakfast tray each morning – also rain or shine, Christmas or August, and onward into complete Neverland. Later, I shifted my dream plan – a split of cold champagne one half hour *before* the tray! Violets, sparkling wine, and trays themselves were as nonexistent as the lover(s), of course, but once again, Why not? By now, I sip a mug of vegetable broth and count myself fortunate, while my mind's nose and eyes feast on the pungency of the purple blossoms, and the champagne stings my sleepy tongue . . . and on feast days I drink a little glass of California 'Dry Sauterne' from the ice box . . . and it is much easier to get out of bed to go to work if there is not that silly tray there.

* * *

Mayonnaise, real mayonnaise, good mayonnaise, is something I can dream of any time, almost, and not because I ate it when I was little but because I did not. My maternal grandmother, whose Victorian neuroses dictated our family table-tastes until I was about twelve, found salads generally suspect, but would tolerate the occasional serving of some watery lettuce in a dish beside each plate (those crescents one still sees now and then in English and Swiss boarding houses and the mansions of American Anglophiles). On it would be a dab or lump or blob, depending on the current cook, of what was quietly referred to as Boiled Dressing. It seemed dreadful stuff – enough to harm one's soul.

I do not have my grandmother's own recipe, although I am sure she scared it into many an illiterate mind in her kitchens, but I have found an approximation, which I feel strangely forced to give. It is from Miss Parloa's 'New Cook Book,' copyrighted in Boston in 1880 by Estes and Lauriat:

Three eggs, one tablespoonful each of sugar, oil and salt, a scant tablespoonful of mustard, a cupful of milk and one of vinegar. Stir oil, mustard, salt and sugar in a bowl until perfectly smooth. Add the eggs, and beat well; then add the vinegar, and finally the milk. Place the bowl in a basin of boiling water, and stir the dressing until it thickens like soft custard. . . .

The dressing will keep two weeks if bottled tightly and put in a cool place.

On second thought, I think Grandmother's receipt, as I am sure it was called, may have used one egg instead of three, skimped on the sugar and oil, left out the mustard, and perhaps eliminated the milk as well. It was a kind of sour whitish gravy and . . . Yes! Patience is its own reward; I have looked in dozens of cookbooks without finding her abysmal secret, and now I have it: she did not use eggs at all, but *flour*. That is it. Flour thickened the vinegar – no need to waste eggs and sugar . . . Battle Creek frowned on oil, and she spent yearly periods at that health resort . . . mustard was a heathen spice . . . salt was cheap, and good cider vinegar came by the gallon . . . And (here I can hear words as clearly as I can see the limp wet lettuce under its load of Boiled Dressing) 'Salad is roughage and a French idea.'

As proof of the strange hold childhood remembrance has on us, I think I am justified to print once, and only once, my considered analysis of the reason I must live for the rest of my life with an almost painful craving for mayonnaise made with fresh eggs and lemon juice and good olive oil:

GRANDMOTHER'S BOILED DRESSING
1 cup cider vinegar.
Enough flour to make thin paste.
Salt to taste.

Mix well, boil slowly fifteen minutes or until done, and serve with wet shredded lettuce.

Unlike any recipe I have ever given, this one has not been tested and never shall be, nor is it recommended for anything but passing thought.

Some of the foods that are of passionate interest in childhood, as potently desirable as drink to a toper, with time lose everything but a cool intellectuality. For about three years, when I was around six, we sometimes ate hot milk toast for Sunday-night supper, but made with rich cocoa, and I would start waiting for the next time as soon as I had swallowed the last crumbly buttery brown spoonful of it. I am thankful I need have no real fear of ever being faced with another bowl of the stuff, but equally happy that I can still understand how its warmth and savor satisfied my senses then. I feel much the same grateful relief when I conjure, no matter how seldom, the four or five years when I was in boarding schools and existed – sensually, at least – from one private slow orgy of saltines and Hershey bars to the next.

There is one concoction, or whatever it should be called, that I was never allowed to eat, and that I dreamed of almost viciously for perhaps seventeen years, until I was about twenty-two and married. I made it then and ate every bit of it and enjoyed it enormously and have never tasted it since, except in the happy reaches of my gastronomical mind. And not long ago, when I found a distinctly literary reference to it, I beamed and glowed. I love the reality of Mark Twain almost as much as I love the dream-image of this dish, and when he included it, just as I myself would have, in a list of American foods he planned to eat –'a modest, private affair,' all to himself – I could hardly believe the miraculous coincidence: my ambrosia, my god's!

In 'A Tramp Abroad,' Twain grouses about the food he found in Europe in 1878 (even a god can sound a little limited at times), and makes a list of the foods he has missed the most and most poignantly awaits on his return. It starts out 'Radishes,' which is indeed either blind or chauvinistic, since I myself always seem to eat five times as many of them when I am a tramp abroad as when I am home. He then names eighty separate dishes, and ends, 'All sorts of American pastry. Fresh American Fruits . . . Ice water.' Love is *not* blind, and I do feel sorry about a certain lack of divinity in this utterance, but my faith and loyalty are forever strengthened by items 57 and 58: 'Mashed Potatoes. Catsup.'

These two things were printed on the same line, and I feel – in fact, I *know* – that he meant 'Mashed potatoes *and* Catsup,' or perhaps 'Mashed potatoes *with* Catsup.' This certainty springs from the fact that there is, in my own mind and plainly in his, an affinity there. The two belong together. I have known this since I was about five, or perhaps even younger. I have proved it – only once, but very thoroughly. I am willing to try to again, preferably in 'a modest, private affair, all to myself,' but in public if I should ever be challenged.

We often ate mashed potatoes at home. Grandmother liked what my mother secretly scoffed at as 'slip-and-go-easies': custards, junkets, strained stewed tomatoes, things like that, with mashed potatoes, of course, at the head of the list as a necessity alongside any decent cut of meat. But – and here is the secret, perhaps, of my life-long craving – we were never allowed to taste catsup. Never. It was spicy and bad for us, and 'common' in bottles.

(This is an odd fact, chronologically, for all the house-keepers of my beldam's vintage prided themselves on their special receipts for 'ketchups,' made of everything from oysters to walnuts and including the plentiful love apple.)

I remember that once when Grandmother was gone off to a religious convention, Mother asked each of us what we would most like to eat before the awesome Nervous Stomach took over our menus again. My father immediately said he would pick a large salad of water-cress from the Rio Hondo and make a dressing of olive oil and wine vinegar – a double cock-snoot, since olive oil was an exotic smelly stuff kept only to rub on the navels of the new babies that seemed to arrive fairly often, and watercress grew along the banks of a stream that might well be . . . er . . . *used* by cows. When my turn came, I said, 'Mashed potatoes and catsup.' I forget exactly what went on next, except that Father was for letting me eat all I wanted of the crazy mixture and I never did get to. Ah, well . . . I loved watercress, too, and whatever other forbidden fruits we bit into during that and similar gastric respites, and I did not need to stop dreaming.

My one deliberate challenge to myself was delicious. I was alone, which seems to be indicated for many such sensual rites. The potatoes were light, whipped to a firm cloud with rich hot milk, faintly yellow from ample butter. I put them in a big warmed bowl, made a dent about the size of a respectable coffee cup, and filled it to the brim with catsup from a large, full, *vulgar* bottle that stood beside my table mat where a wineglass would be at an ordinary, commonplace, everyday banquet. Mine was, as I have said, delicious. I would, as I have also said, gladly do it again if I were dared to. But I prefer to nourish myself with the knowledge that it is not impossible (potato chips), not too improbable (fresh Beluga caviar). And now I am sharing it with a friend. I could not manage to serve forth to Mark Twain the 'Sheephead and croakers, from New Orleans,' or the 'Prairie hens, from Illinois,' that he dreamed of in European boarding houses ninety years ago, but mashed potatoes *with* catsup are ready to hand when he says the word.

Love in a Dish

Brillat-Savarin, who amused himself in his old age by writing *The Physiology of Taste*, a book which, after almost 125 years of near idolatry and countless imitators, remains the wittiest and wisest of its kind, concerned himself mightily with the problem of married bliss. He wrote many paragraphs and pages on the importance of gastronomy in love, and told a dozen anecdotes which in one or another of his slyly subtle ways proved the point, put bluntly, that happiness at table leads to happiness in bed.

A mutual enjoyment of the pleasures of the table, he said over and over, has an enormous influence on the felicity that can and should be found in marriage. A couple, he went on, who can share this enjoyment 'have, at least once every day, a delightful reason for being together, for even those who sleep in separate beds (and there are many such in 1825) at least eat at the same table; they have an unfailing subject of conversation; they can talk not only of what they are eating, but also of what they have eaten before and will eat later, and of what they have noticed in other dining rooms, of fashionable new recipes and dishes, etc., etc.: everyone knows that such intimate chit-chat is full of its own charms.'

Brillat-Savarin felt, and said so strongly, that a man

and woman who share any such basic need as the one for food will be eager to please and amuse each other in the satisfying of that need, and will do what they can to make the basically animal process enjoyable. 'And the way in which mealtimes are passed,' he wrote firmly, 'is most important to what happiness we find in life.'

Of course, this observation was not original with the old French lawyer. Chinese philosophers made it in much the same words three thousand years ago, and any thoughtful psychiatrist will make it today, when our boulevards are lined with an infinity of bad eating houses filled with dead-faced people placed like mute beasts in their stalls; today, when one out of every three marriages ends in divorce.

It seems incredible that normal human beings not only tolerate the average American restaurant food, but actually prefer it to eating at home. The only possible explanation for such deliberate mass-poisoning, a kind of suicide of the spirit as well as the body, is that meals in the intimacy of a family dining-room or kitchen are unbearable.

At a drugstore counter, backed by trusses wrapped in cellophane and faced by wavy-haired young men dressed like dental assistants, conversation is unnecessary if not quite impossible.

Nagging and whining are temporarily shut off, and a married man and woman can sit side by side like strangers.

At home, fatigue and boredom would sour the words they spoke and the food they ate, and the words would be hateful and the food would be dull as ditchwater and drearily served forth. The monotony of preparing meals which evoke no sign of pleasure would have knocked the woman into a rut of glum can-opening, the man into dour acceptance. Anything is better than being penned together in one room, having to chew and breathe in unison, they feel. And they go, in a kind of wordless dread of being alone, to this Broiler, that Chili-Heaven.

And having failed so completely to satisfy in harmony one of their three basic needs, it cannot be wondered that the other two, for love and shelter, are increasingly unfulfilled. There can be no warm, rich home-life anywhere else if it does not exist at table, and in the same way there can be no enduring family happiness, no real *marriage*, if a man and woman cannot open themselves generously and without suspicion one to the other over a shared bowl of soup as well as a shared caress.

I do not know many people very well, but I am on terms of close friendship with at least three families, this very minute, who worry me greatly because they are increasingly unhappy at table – and, therefore, everywhere. It is true that things have conspired against them to make the quiet little dinners of courtship impossible: children and wars and worries have pushed the candlelight and the leisure far into the past. But it seems to me that a lack of understanding on the part of the husbands is the real trouble.

* * *

The wives, whether consciously or not, have remembered the French adage that good cooking is like love, needing both tact and variety. They have tried, not always too successfully, to make meals that were exciting and amusing. The response from their husbands, almost unfailingly, has been, 'What's all this fancy stuff? Give me good plain food, will you? I'm strictly a steak-and-potato boy, honey! And for God's sake remember it!'

Once spoken to this way, a woman, who feels instinctively that cooking is one of her last resorts as a creative outlet, withdraws, rebuffed and hurt. She still manages to make something of a reputation for herself as a 'party cook,' and serves elaborate curries and heavily flavored desserts which annoy her politely silent mate. In between 'company' she sincerely believes that she is trying to please him by a monotonous series of steak-and-potato dinners, although there is increasing resentment in her subconscious mind against his noncommittal acceptance of what he must surely know is boring to her.

He, on his part, may sense a disappointment in her, may feel that he has let her down in some way which he does not bother to analyze, and he covers his uncomfortable self-doubt by added silence. The result is that meals for the two of them grow more and more strained. He never comments on the food, because he knows just what there will be and what it will taste like, and if he is Anglo-Saxon he has probably been raised to think of such conversation as bad manners or at least foolish.

She, knowing that she can expect no fine fillip of a compliment, takes less interest every day in ordering and preparing the food, and finally grows so revolted by it and all it has come to stand for in her feeling toward her husband that she cannot eat properly. She grows nervous and tires easily.

Finally, with unspoken relief, they begin to dine

oftener in public places, where at first the unaccustomed noise and movement and the new flavors make meals seem a pleasure again. They talk and drink and eat gaily, and go home to more happiness than for a long time.

Soon, though, they become accustomed to one or two restaurants, where they always order the same things and are served by the same waiters. They have less and less to say. The man eats hungrily at his steak, satisfying his need for nourishment in a way which he has been led to believe is a proof of his virility, or at least masculinity. 'No fancy stuff for me,' he says. 'Good meat, that's all a man needs – good meat and potatoes and plenty of it, and you can have all these sauces and courses and this and that. Take too much time! All right for parties, I guess . . .'

If he sees that his wife, sitting across from him in the cafe, has the blank, peaked look on her face which he has come to dread in bed, he may worry about her and tell her that she should eat more honest-to-God food, instead of all those salads. She may smile at him. And she may not.

* * *

Perhaps the two of them should read or re-read Brillat-Savarin's book. In it he would make clear to them that a healthy interest in the pleasures of the table, the gastronomical art, can bring much happiness. They would see the stupidity of asserting one's virility by a diet limited to the needs of a dog or lion, and the silliness of proving one's interest in exotic living by over-spiced indigestible messes.

In Richardson Wright's *Bed-Book of Eating and Drinking*, he wrote in a discussion of the delights of supping in the kitchen, that more meals served on oilcloth by the stove might be one way to 'stabilize our American marital status. I hold to the lowly belief,' he went on, 'that a man never knows the sureness of being happily married until he has . . . cooked a meal himself.'

Brillat-Savarin believed much the same thing, and made it plain that gentlemen of unquestioned masculinity among his friends found added vigor and zest for life's pleasures in the kitchen, where they could pit their skill and intelligence against the laws of nature and more often than not emerge triumphantly with a roasted quail or a soufflé to prove their point.

I shiver with sadness for my drifting friends, when I read in the *Bed-Book* (Mr. Wright has but paraphrased the old Frenchman, which is almost inevitable in anything connected with gastronomy) 'The first sign of marital trouble is when a man or woman finds it distasteful to face each other at table . . . I am convinced that a man and wife with congenial appetites and a knowledge of foods and cooking have the basis for lasting happiness.'

The French have perhaps written more than any people but the Chinese about food as well as love. (Another of them has said, 'A man is captured through his heart, but is held captive forever through his stomach!') But it is not a Gallic prerogative and I have as much right as any other thoughtful and affectionate person to decide for my friends that if they were happier at table they would be happier elsewhere.

Any such state can be attained deliberately, if done with intelligence, but once attained it must be nurtured with constant attention. The man must try to understand what it is about making a curry or a bouillabaisse that lightens his wife's face and heart. The woman must try to understand why a husband needs to bolster his preconceptions of virility now and then with a bit of reactionary conservatism. He must use his brain at home as well as at his office, and decide that cultivating his palate is at least as important as perfecting his golf-stroke. She must read and think, until she can conclude for herself that a heavy hand with the condiments is no guarantee of a culinary escape from boredom.

* * *.

Then and only then, they will find that they can face each other warmly and gaily across the table again, and that even steak-and-potatoes, when they have been prepared with a shared interest and humor and intelligence, can be one great pleasure which leads to another, and perhaps – who knows – an even greater one.

Two Kitchens in Provence

PREFACE

Anything can be a lodestar in a person's life, I suppose, and for some fortunates like me, the Kitchen serves well. Often the real influence of a lodestar is half understood, or partly unsuspected, but with a little reflection it grows clear to me that kitchens have always played a mysterious part in my shaping.

Since I wrote about two of them I knew when I stayed several years in Provence, I have known two more in that fair country, in Aix and Marseille. Like the first ones, they are vivid in my recollections, each with its own smells, its own views onto the world and into myself.

The one in Marseille, in 1973 I think, was perhaps the least dignified of any of a long lifetime of them. It was part of a miserable little bathroom: a two-burner gas plate beside the washbowl, a saucepan and a soup pot on the shelf for toothpaste and combs. To pretend to bathe in the small scarred tub, which never ran anything but tepid water whether it came from the hot spigot or the cold, my sister and I had to duck under the sagging string that held our dish and face towels. Above the spigots there was a high window perhaps ten inches square, which we had to stand in the tub to open or close. It opened onto a dim air well, so that we knew intimate things about our unseen neighbors.

But past this dreadful cell were two big airy rooms with good red tiles on the floor, with a big window in each room looking far down on one of the most exciting places in the world, the Old Port of Marseille, and then far out to sea, far up into the blanched cruel hills. For part of the months we lived there, rapt by all we saw, we could watch the sun both rise and set, so high and wide were the windows. We never stopped looking, except when we slept lightly through the night-sounds of police sirens, small ships, bugles blowing in the barracks across the street, now and then a band rehearsing on the empty sidewalks for some celebration.

We ate as close as possible to one of the windows, shut against the mistral, open to the warm sun. The foul little bath-kitchen produced miracles of good plain food from its two pans, and we bought some plates and bowls of Provençal pottery, and two sturdy wineglasses, so that everything tasted even better. Salads were easy. So was good *café au lait*, and we soon learned where to find the most commendable croissants, the most pungent mountain honey. We could get local cheeses, and homemade *pâtés* sent to our shopkeepers by cousins in Normandy or Alsace. Now and then we bought a little roasted chicken from an elegant catering shop on the Rue de Rome. And the *vins rosés* were ever-flowing . . .

The kitchen in Aix-en-Provence, a couple of years later, was nothing but a counter in the single room, with a shoddy little 'frigidaire' at one end and a small dauntless water heater at the other, and a typical hideous sink in the middle, like the first two I had known in that part of the country: scooped from a slab of gritty brown marble and completely inadequate for anything at all that one has to do in a kitchen sink. Like the others, it was probably at least two hundred years old, made in the days of pitchers and pails and open drains, not meant to have water splashing into it from a tap . . .

Again I was with my sister, and again we found a big airy room to live in, twice the size of the two in Marseille, and on the second storey instead of the ninth. There was no view this time, but the sky and its wheeling whistling swallows was close to us. The floor was of red tiles, of course, and we could keep a few pots of geraniums in the windows, since we were on a narrow street out of the mistral's way.

The fruits and vegetables of Aix were, as always, picked at dawn and meant to be eaten by nightfall. It was exciting once more to find myself racing decay, as I had learned to do at Le Tholonet and then L'Harmas. A peach bought cool and unblemished from the greengrocer on the Cours Sextius at nine in the morning looked sulky by noon, and by suppertime was bruised and voluptuously dying. The bright yellow blossoms on courgettes from the Marché aux Herbes had wilted by noon, and the first waxy glow of the slender squashes was gone by the time they made our supper. But eggs and unsalted butter stayed fresh in the miserable little icebox, and the wine was always cool.

That time in Aix, there was a rebirth of local pride, and along with the clean restoration of beautiful old façades and courtyards there was a new interest in regional cooking, so that we could buy excellent breads and cheeses and *pâtés* from a dozen somewhat artsy 'caves' and 'boutiques.'

In Marseille, not long before, we had eaten well but in a limited way in our flat, and had satisfied more than our basic hungers in many restaurants both great and small. In Aix we ate better food in our one-room flat than we could find in the town. We had perhaps four pans and kettles instead of two, and could braise little quails for a treat, or make a lusty ratatouille, or even a dainty omelet . . . and of course it was pleasant not to have to push aside the toothpaste to find the forks and spoons.

In Marseille we had ushered in the Free Market vegetables and fruits being shipped enthusiastically, if without experience, from Israel and Portugal, which in their dried-out, half-ripe, half-frozen state were almost nostalgically like the California supermarket produce my sister and I had hoped to escape. Every time we went by bus from Marseille to Aix, which happened more often as we bowed to our helpless devotion to the town, we brought back *good* things to eat. We felt disloyal, because we loved the city too. But it was better than ever to sit by one of the big windows above the Old Port and eat *real* green beans instead of the ersatz half-dead things for sale in Marseille.

And in the flat in Aix it was good to sit by one of the big windows and pretend we were looking down at the Old Port instead of across at a line of dripping red and pink laundry hung from a neighbor's kitchen out over the street. Perhaps the fish of Aix was eighteen miles older than in Marseille, we agreed, but its radishes were

as fresh and delicate as dewdrops . . . the cherries were
as crisp as new almonds . . .

It is fortunate to recognize lodestars as such. They
light our paths, and shape us mysteriously, and in the
process can teach true humility. How and why, I now ask
myself, have I known not one or two but four kinds of
kitchens of Provence?

I

I have had two kitchens in Provence. The first was above
the empty stables at the Château du Tholonet, about five
miles easterly from Aix, near the village of Le Tholonet.
My two young girls and I were living there for a few
months in 1956, before we had to leave, after a long stay,
for America and home.

The kitchen was about nine by nine feet, with a ceil-
ing fourteen feet high and a window looking west toward
Aix, over two rolling meadows bright with scarlet poppies and sweet grasses and then to the slopes of the
Châteaunoir, covered with humming pine woods. It was
one of the best kitchens I ever worked in, although it
was inefficient, inadequate, and often filled with flies.

The walls were plastered stone. There was a hood
built into the east wall over a low platform with three
grates in it. A long time ago, this had served as a stove
for the grooms and stableboys who slept and ate there
above the carriages and horses of the château, and now
a small white enamel butane stove sat with an air of
embarrassed practicality upon its red tiles. Behind it was a
black iron plaque about three feet square, of a wild-haired

hero whipping a giant lizard – St. Michael, no doubt, worsting his dragon. I forget the antiquarian name for these iron chimney guards; they were used to protect the soft chimney stones against the steady blaze on such hearths, which all kitchens once kept hot and bright.

To the right of the hearth, by the window, which looked down on a fast brooklet and a rocky path where the shepherd led his flock each night and morning, was a marble sink with a tap that now ran water, now did not, depending on what the farmer was doing in his garden. It was a shallow oval hollow in a slab of the local stone quarried up behind us in Bibémus, where Cézanne used to roam and struggle with his vision of what light is made of. When there was water and I used it, I always kept it as clean as I could, for it splashed out directly from the hole in the wall onto the shepherd's path twenty feet below. The sink was faced with the same red tiles as the old stove and the floor – the rough glazed squares of red and pink and ochre clay that comes from the soil of Provence, the clay that makes the roofs there glow and burn even in the moonlight. They were cool in summer, warm and comforting in winter, and easy to clean, and altogether so pleasing that the prospect of ever having to walk about on another surface was painful to me. Except for the tiles, the kitchen was whitewashed. There were three shelves above the drab little sink, which was reinstated several times a day in my favor because it had, if I wished to go into the bathroom and light a heater, hot as well as cold water. Or perhaps I esteemed it merely because it had water at all.

There was a worn pine table, on which I kept a clay

water pitcher, and the wine bottles, and a wicker tray for the vegetables, and a reed satchel filled with rapidly staling bread. Then there was a shallow high cupboard with screen doors, where I kept everything that was not on the table and the sink shelves – food, plates, the rare leftovers, tubes of mustard and concentrates. I had very little equipment. I had borrowed two pans and a skillet, and I made a pleasurable investment in Provençal pottery casseroles, plates, and bowls. The Monoprix solved in a fortunately temporary way the problem of decent knives and forks and spoons, except for one viciously beautiful all-purpose blade.

Downstairs, in the enormous, echoing stone carriage room through which we passed to our ironwork stairway, was a little wire-screen box in which I was supposed to safeguard things. But in Provence food spoils very quickly, and except for a few hard-rock sausages and green bananas, which I left down there, I found it simpler to buy the minimum of butter and so on and keep it upstairs in the kitchen cupboard.

I took a while to get into what is basically an easy rhythm of marketing, and a couple of times I found myself facing one withered lemon, a boiled potato, and a bowl of subtly rotten green beans for supper. Alone, I would have gone to bed with the latest edition of a Georges Simenon, but with my little girls Anne and Mary there, it seemed providential that the Restaurant Thomé was only a quarter mile away. We would walk down past the château and its tranquil ponds of water, teeming in the late spring with still speechless froglets, and under the rows of trimmed and untrimmed giant

71

plane trees, and across the bridge above the lively little river, and there would be the welcome, as it had been for almost a hundred and fifty years – the smiling owner, his nice wife, all her sisters and brothers, and always a new baby somewhere under an impeccable mosquito net. Perhaps the fancy electric spit would be turning a few pullets for a big country wedding tomorrow, tablecloths would be fluttering in the garden, and not a sound now from the discreet little viny pergolas where Prince Edward and his less noble but equally gallant imitators used to entertain their traveling companions.

There was a bus that zoomed through the village three mornings a week, on market days in Aix, and at least once weekly my girls and I hopped it, at five minutes after nine. At the markets, we would fill the two string bags we carried with us, and the two or three woven baskets, all bulging with hard vegetables at the bottom and things like wood strawberries on top, and head for our favorite taxi at the top of the Cours Mirabeau, picking up packages along the way – a square of Dijon gingerbread and a pot of Alpine honey at the little 'health-food store' on the Place Forbin, an onion tart for a treat at the pastry shop on the Rue Thiers, a bottle of vermouth at the Caves Phocéennes. We would be loaded to the gunwales, full of hope that we had purchased enough for another week.

In a short time, I learned that I was lugging things home from Aix that I could get in the village, and then only occasionally did I find myself with either too much, all withering and spoiling, or nothing at all and no bus for two days and the store in the Relai de Cézanne (the

store is the other half of the old café-inn where Cézanne
often stopped when he was painting along the Route du
Tholonet) in Le Tholonet, across from the Restaurant
Thomé, closed because of a wedding-funeral-christening –
or just closed. (I soon found that on Mondays it always
was.) I knew that the good bread from Palette, which
leaned like fat and thin bean poles in a big basket in the
corner, was fresh on Tuesdays and Saturdays, and that
on those days I could usually buy some milk and butter.
Saturday mornings, there would always be a few crates of
fresh vegetables. I could buy, for instance, little artichokes,
new potatoes, carrots, courgettes, tomatoes, bananas;
bread and butter and milk, of course, and some Gruyère
cheese; a couple of soup sausages; and a copy of the
weekly Mickey comics for the children. In the middle of
the week, though, the stock at the store might consist
of some dusty packages of noodles, a few big cubes of
yellow laundry soap, and penny caramels for the twenty-
eight children of the school district.

In addition to the store, there were several little trucks
that came regularly up the narrow roads from the
national highway at Palette. On Wednesdays, the butcher
drove right up to the front of the château, blowing his
horn long and merry, and the shepherdess would come
from the beautiful stone barns, where she lived with her
husband and two hundred sheep, several rams, two
goats, three astonishing sheep dogs, and forty chickens
and four pigs; the farmer's wife would come from the
wing of the beautiful hollow stone château, where she
lived with her husband and a little abandoned child they
had saved; the gardener's wife would come up from the

73

beautiful gate cottage; the miller's wife and mother would come down from the beautiful stone house in the mill beside the waterfall behind the château; and I would come from the beautiful stone stables. We would watch one another's purchases and spendings casually, and talk in a somewhat artificial overcordial but friendly way about whose children had whooping cough and whose had chicken pox and whether it would rain, while the suave young butcher, with the remote, weary face of a night clerk in a cheap hotel, cut deftly into his slabs of meat, and weighed out black and green olives, cheese, and marbled lard. Gradually, we would go back under the chestnut trees and the plane trees to our kitchens, and he would drive away, to return Sunday at noon, when he would stop in front of the water pump in the village and blare his horn commandingly to the people returning from Mass and sitting in front of the Relai with their milky *pastis* in front of them on the little tables.

Fridays at Le Tholonet, a small fish jeep tooted in, with an old cornet cracking out its jaunty message, past the tranquil straight ponds in the front of the château. By the time it got there, only a few fish would be left, but they were still fresh, and usually good. All Mediterranean fish seem much stronger in their smells and flavors than those of colder waters. Once, I remember, I bought the tail end of a large silvery one with a tough skin and a big backbone, and it sent off quite a fume from the beginning, although not at all a tired or suspicious one. I rubbed it with olive oil, put some thin slices of lemon on it, and poured about a cupful of white wine over it in a shallow casserole. Then, instead of allowing fifteen minutes as the fisherman had advised, I baked it for about a half hour in a gentle oven, which was the only kind I had – the two burners on top of the little stove on the hearth were almost too lively, but the oven never worked up much enthusiasm.

That was the night we tried a package of dried mushroom soup that the Aix grocer had given me to prove that such innovations could be good, and we enjoyed the smooth, well-seasoned creamy mixture so much that we decided to eat the fish cold the next day, with a mayonnaise I would make with an egg from the shepherdess and a plastic gadget I had bought some time before from a very fat man in a chef's bonnet, who was showing at a little table in the market how it could be done in twenty seconds with never a failure. I put the fish back in the cool oven, and the next morning took it out to skin and bone, when I heard the postman's whistle at the château. Quickly, I covered the casserole with the breadboard and a towel, to protect the fish from flies, and went over to talk with him about if and how I could register a letter without going in to Aix.

On the way back, Whisky, our guest poodle, who came three miles by himself every day or so from the Château-noir to amuse us and sample our cuisine before he puffed up the hill again to his real home, dashed away from me, through the stables and up our long flight of stone stairs in the dim coach house. Just as I got to the bottom of them, the biggest black cat I ever saw, and one I had certainly never seen before, whipped down past me and then out the enormous door, with Whisky yapping nobly at a safe distance.

Of course, the kitchen was a shambles. That stranger cat had caught, perhaps from miles away, the pungent invitation of my baked fishtail. He had come to it as unerringly as one rare insect in a jungle finds his only possible mate. He had snatched open the cupboard door, which was too warped to latch shut, and had fiercely tossed to the floor everything unfishy. Then he had slapped his way through the wastebasket. Finally, he had clawed off the heavy breadboard and towel from the casserole and he had dragged and flapped the whole oily, dripping mess down onto the red tile floor, where, from the look of things, he had not only torn the meat to small bits but rolled in it. So we did not have to try out the mayonnaise gadget for a while longer.

Saturday afternoons, there was always the visit of the rolling *épicerie*, with things like shoelaces, aspirin, custard powders, and boxes of cookies with bright-pink frosting on them and names like Bébés Délices or Nounous de Titi. The man who jolted it around that rocky country had a good face, like a tired village doctor or lawyer. Usually I would need almost nothing, but I would buy two lemons, perhaps, or a piece of good soft-firm reblochon cheese from the Savoy – the kind that the houseman I had when I was living in Switzerland used to smuggle dramatically across the Lake of Geneva in a rowboat on dark nights and sell at a high sum to me and other dupes in Vevey. It tasted just as good from the back of a beat-up old grocery truck in Provence.

We always added the lemons to the artichokes and the tomatoes and the other vegetables I kept on the wicker tray, in vague memory of a still life seen somewhere with

the same whitewashed walls for background, and we
would eat most of the cheese for supper after big bowls
of the broth from the soup – the sausage soup, which
seemed to be standard in that part of the country and
which I soon grew to make almost automatically, like the
other housewives. The sausages were lean, dry things,
and were boiled whole with whatever vegetables were at
hand and then either sliced into the broth or fished out
and eaten cold the next day with bread.

I could agree with all the women living in that wild,
beautiful country only five miles from Aix and less than
two from the screaming Nice-Marseille highway and
with three buses to the market a week: it was good to
hear the brave, bright, insistent horn-blowing and know
that there would be food for our families. And it was
good, in a way hard to explain even to myself, after years
of deep-freeze and run-of-the-mill marketing in California, to know that, willy-nilly, the fish would spoil by
tomorrow, the chops would be practically incandescent
in thirty-six hours, and the tomatoes would rot in twelve.
It was a kind of race between my gluttony for the fine
freshness and my knowledge of its fleeting nature.

To cope with this inescapable rapidity of decay in a
warm, bacteria-rich, fly-infested ancient land without
any means of cooling except the stone cellars and wells,
I kept a small supply of canned vegetables and fruits,
and the omnipresent and very handy tubes of everything
from salmon butter to various good mustards to concen-
trated milk and tomato sauce. Then I had on hand several
packages of those ugly but valuable soup powders (potato-
and-leek, chicken-consommé, fish), which I found made

good sauces, too, in a pinch. I had wonderful olive oil, ladled into my bottle from an unctuous vat in Aix that I would not mind being shipped home in, instead of malmsey, and good gutty red-wine vinegar, and I could go up to the farmer's garden whenever I wanted to for tough but delicious salads. Salt is a lot saltier in Provence than at home, and less refined; the pepper is called 'grey' and has an overtaste of turpentine, somewhat like the berries I used to chew when they dropped from the feathery pepper trees when I was a little girl in California. And then, of course, there were things that most tin-can cooks have in any modern country: sardines, anchovies, Alsatian sauerkraut for a moment of gastronomical debauchery for my children, one little can of lark *pâté* for me – complete with the first French can opener I had ever been able to work, which I paid rather a lot for in the cutlery shop across from the Palais de Justice.

With the mistral surging and leaning against the windows and the chestnut trees and the red poppies in the meadows, and the spiritual food a part of the whole, we would eat at breakfast canned grapefruit juice, large bowls of *café au lait* with brown sugar, slices of Dijon gingerbread with sweet butter and Alpine honey; at noontime whole new potatoes boiled in their jackets in a big pot of carrots-onions-sausage, which we'd eat later, sweet butter, mild cheese, and a bowl of green olives and little radishes; then for supper the vegetable broth, with the sausage cut in thin rings, the whole new carrots and onions drained and tossed with a little butter and chopped parsley and celery tops from the farmer's garden, and a bowl of three cans mixed together of peaches-pears-pineapple, all with hot, delicious, somewhat charcoalish toast made on one of those flat grill things our parents used at least forty years ago. The next day, there would still be some clear broth, and I would make a jelly from the fruit juices. And I would start over again – probably a big salad, which I would soak in the fountain to rid it of most of the innumerable critters that are considered correct for country produce in Provence, and then a pot of hot small artichokes to eat with melted butter and lemon juice, and sliced tomatoes that had lasted two days after marketing instead of only one because the mistral was blowing, and then maybe soft-boiled eggs from the shepherdess for supper.

There was always that little rich decadent tin of lark *pâté* in the cupboard if I grew bored, or we could stroll down past the great ponds under the plane trees to the deft, friendly welcome of the Restaurant Thomé and eat a grilled pullet or a trout *meunière*, and an orange baked *à la norvégienne*. Or we could stay home and I would try at last the mayonnaise maker I had bought from the fat man in the market.

II

The second kitchen I had in Provence, when we lived in a part of an old farmhouse at L'Harmas, about three miles from Aix on the Route du Tholonet, was somewhat different from the one at the château a few years before. There was much more luxury. There was a small noisy electric refrigerator called, as everywhere in the world – except, perhaps, America – a 'frigidaire.' There was an imitation-modern white enamel stove with an oven and four burners. Two of the burners always blew out at once, so, except for the oven, which could not be adjusted to anything but a blasting roar and which I never used, I was just as before, in the older kitchen at the château, with the portable two-burner butane stove. There was the same slab of hollowed marble for a sink, with a round instead of oval basin scooped in it, but it had two taps, which usually had water in them, and quite often there was hot water without my having to light anything, unless someone had taken a bath in the past twelve hours, or there was a drought, or the farm pump was out of order. And there were several more shelves, for dishes and pots.

Two windows, not so high from the ground as in the kitchen over the stables, gave upon a terrace shaded by the tall trees of that country, which must bend to the mistral and shed their branches almost to their tops – a little like the wild pines in Monterey in California, but higher and thinner. The terrace was half wild, too, and could be deep in voluptuous sweet grasses and flowers in the spring, or dry and stinging with pointy weeds, or almost bare until the snow brought soft rains again. It heartened me to watch it and to smell its changing wildness as I stood in the kitchen, using it for its destined purpose – to feed people near me.

The food was the same in both kitchens; it dared me daily. But I must go to Aix for everything this time, for the jeeps and trucks that had come to the château did not seem to come this near the big town. I must get to the open markets and to a few little shops, and then on home, *fast*, before things spoiled. I went on foot. I did not want to have a car; it was too rare a thing to miss, that walking along the little Route du Tholonet – Cézanne's road – in all weathers, against all tides, between the farm and Aix. I rose very early to head for town, carrying a nest of the light straw baskets that the Gypsies still wove, and then bringing them back full and heavy in a taxi. (There were few paper sacks in that country, and baskets and string bags were uniform.)

The Big Market is held three times a week – on Tuesday, Thursday, and Saturday – but every day, behind the post office, there is the Little Market. Both of them are beautiful and exciting and soothing, a tonic to the senses, but I think I loved the little one more.

The Place Richelme et aux Herbes is small, and shaded by very tall and noble plane trees, which in summer sift down such a green light as I have seldom seen. Perhaps some fortunate fish have known it, but for human beings it is rare to float at the bottom of the deeps and yet breathe with rapture the smells of all the living things spread out to sell in the pure, filtered moving air. There are snails in cages, ducklings bright-eyed in their crates, trembling rabbits. There are baskets of fresh herbs, and little piles of edibles gathered at dawn in a hundred gardens: peas and strawberries in the spring, small cabbages, apples, new potatoes, and onions and garlic, following inexorably the farmers' almanac, so that one soon accustoms the purchases and their uses to the crops that have been sowed and harvested thus for two thousand years at least.

Sometimes there was a man with a tiny donkey, selling baskets of fresh lavender, or crude mint drops from the Pyrenees, or cough lozenges made from Alpine herbs and saps. He always put a ringlet of what he was selling that day over the patient head of his little beast – in hot weather, on her hat. On one corner, behind the beautiful old grain market that now housed harried postal clerks, there was a quiet man with a folding table, making metal nameplates for people's doorways, in every kind of painstaking elaborate lettering. Once, he gave me a tiny ring, cut from a peach stone. It was for *me*, he said without irony, but it would not have fit a newborn babe.

At either end of the little square are small cafés and shops, and opposite the post office is a bleak, busy annex lined with fish markets and shops selling poultry, butter, and all kinds of smoked sausages and hams. Underneath this annex is a well-run and modern public toilet, new since our first stay in Aix and built by the city.

The other market, the big one, is comparatively gigantic, and always very crowded and amusing, but not dream-like, not deep golden green, even in its generous summer shade. I came to know it well, and soon. It is in a long square that is not square at all, with the Palais de Justice on one side, and many small shops and cafés and pharmacies and honorable bookstores and even the Girls' High School fringing it, dominated by the somber, vaguely sinister Church of the Madeleine and – at the time I was there – by two monuments. One of these, the statue of Mirabeau down by the Palais, is now gone. It is said to have been the most ridiculous public monument ever erected in France. This is a broad and daring statement, given the evidence against it, but certainly the small furious figure of Mirabeau, his wig askew and no pockmarks showing, with a knee-high lion cowering against him like a fat poodle, the two shooting up from a stony froth of great-breasted Muses, was very funny, even to the respectful. The monument that remains, the obelisk at the opposite end of the square, is fine indeed, and it rises pure and classical from the fountain at its base, where people dip water for their stalls and the flower women douse their posies.

At the low end of the unsquare square, on the regular Tuesdays, Thursdays, and – especially – Saturdays, is the Flea Market, a reputable debauch of canny snoopers for the great antique dealers of Paris and London and New York, and housewives looking for old wineglasses or copper pans, and happy drifters. Next come the merchants of nails and screws, junk jewelry, clothes, and kitchen stuff – and very few of them are fly-by-nights; most have their regular patrons among people like the farmers and the Algerians, who prefer to shop under open skies. Then there are always a few barkers under umbrellas, selling the kind of paring knife that for them alone will cut everything but the Greek alphabet with a flip of the wrist, or patterns for chic dresses that can be made from four dish towels. Even Bibles.

And then come the real market stalls, the ones where people buy to live. First of all, next to the café where we had long liked to eat couscous occasionally, there was (and probably still is) a woman who sold fresh peanuts in their shells. She was Algerian, I think, or half so, and she had such a delectable texture and color to her skin that I was glad she sold something I could buy from her, in order to talk a little and look at her. She was like a ripe, washed apricot, with the same glowing deep color coming through, as if from far underneath her smooth, tight skin. I have seen such tones in a few faces and in some stained glass in churches. Most of her customers were the thin and thick Algerian women who drifted by twos in their floating flowered dresses along the aisles of the market, and sometimes I listened to her speaking with them in their breathy language. She thought I was very funny, to be so plainly Anglo-Saxon and to be buying peanuts from her.

All the stands were alike and violently different, of course, and the prices were much the same, and the high quality was, too. It seemed to be a question of growing used to one vendor instead of another, and I soon confessed to myself that it was part of the pleasure to be recognized by some of the quick, tough people who carried on that never-ending business. They looked so fresh and strong, three times a week, and I felt flabby and exhausted to think that every day – not just three – they must buy, or grow, and load their wares, and drive to this town or that, and set up their stalls, and then at the end start home again. They were cheerful, and as watchful as cats and as impersonal, and yet they knew most of the people who traded with them, and smiled and joked as if I, or she, or that old woman with no teeth, or the smart young matron in white gloves, were a special pet. 'Ah, how did they remember *me?*' one would ask delightedly, piling the brass weighing bowls higher with the new potatoes round and hard as plums, the stiff buds of artichokes purple and succulent.

Each time I went in to the markets from L'Harmas, I had quite firmly in my mind what we needed for at least two days ahead, what we might need in case of company, and what I would undoubtedly fall heir to or in love with at the last minute – that minute of decision between a good clean rabbit hanging with his own dignity, albeit naked, or some plucked, blackish pigeons I had just spied in the poultry woman's stand. I would start out with three or four empty baskets, and a coin purse full of the small change essential to such hectic purchasing. I would end with heavy baskets and the purse much lighter, of course; money goes fast for food, and even faster for good food, and although I knew better, I always thought in terms of pounds and ounces and I bought in kilos, so that often when I thought I had two pounds of new peas I was toting two kilograms, or more than double what my mind stupidly kept reckoning. Then I would add two kilos of soft, sweet Valencia oranges from Spain, and a half kilo of lemons; two kilos of beans as long as hairpins and not much thicker; two kilos of country tomatoes, smaller and more pungent than the big handsome ones from up near Avignon; a smoked sausage, the kind still packed into clean, uneven gut skin instead of smooth plastic; some cheese; a last generous basket of dead-ripe gooseberries; a kilo of fresh spaghetti from the fat woman by the fountain; and a clumsy bunch of pale-pink carnations: 'Five dozen for two francs today – take advantage, my pretty ladies.'

I would be hot, harried, and overladen. Down on the wide shady Cours Mirabeau, which, perhaps rightly, has been called the most beautiful Main Street in the

world, there are taxis. I would push toward them. The
peanut woman smiled always at me with gaiety and some
mockery – she so solid and ripe and apricot brown, I so
tottery and foreign – and I would feel stronger for her
casual warmth. And under the trees of the Cours, Fern-
and or Michel would take all my baskets and then me into
his taxi for the drive out along Cézanne's road, toward
home.

Sometimes I would want him to go faster, for I could
almost feel the food in the baskets swelling with juice,
growing soft, splitting open in an explosive rush toward
ripeness and disintegration. The fruits and vegetables of
Provence are dying as they grow – literally leaping from
the ancient soil, so filled with natural richnesses and
bacilli and fungi that they seem a kind of summing up of
whatever they *are*. A tomato there, for instance, is the
essence of all tomatoes, of tomato-ness, the way a frag-
ment from a Greek frieze is not a horse but *horse* itself.

As soon as I got back from the markets, I always reor-
ganized everything I had gleaned, as fast as I could,
against the onslaughts of time (especially summer time)
and insects. First of all, there were the flies. The flies of
Provence are said to be the most audacious in the world.
People have remarked on this for at least twenty-five
hundred years, and I have read that slaves being led in
chains from the north to man the galleys anchored at
Toulon marched fastest on this last lap of their death trip
because of the flies that goaded them. Flourishing
descendants of those foul, hungry insects still zigzag in
a year-round dance there, especially in spring and summer, or perhaps autumn, and the grim acceptance of

them is one of the requirements of life, especially on farms, where the soil itself is an age-old amalgam of droppings from beast and man. They were much worse at the château, of course, for there we lived close to the barns, where the shepherd kept all his sheep-goats-chickens-rabbits, and at least three or four pigs, in a timeless, fruity muck that must surely have glowed in the dark. At L'Harmas, there were only pigeons and two peacocks, but there was fine shade in the summer for the flies of that hillside, and warmth in the winter, and the general interest to be found in four families of two-legged creatures.

The ants are almost as powerful in Provence as the flies, surging relentlessly from the red earth, seeming to walk through wood and stone and metal and glass toward whatever they want. And there are other pests that like the cool tiled floors, or the dark of cupboards, or the moist dimness under old drains: scorpions, centi-pedes, bees, and wasps, earwigs, crickets, several kinds of gnats, now and then a snail or a tick. It was the flies and the ants I tilted with first and constantly, and I do not think I disliked them the most because they *were* the most but because I hated and still hate the sound and feel of flies, and the smell of ants. We are at odds always. Sometimes I can acknowledge their complacency – they will be here long after I have made my final stand against them.

In the part of the farmhouse where we lived at L'Harmas, there was a dim room that had once been a buttery, or even the farmer's office, I think. It had an uneven tiled floor, two windows with the shutters left bowed to form a kind of airy cooler, an old piano with no wires in it, and several hooks let into the plastered stone walls. From these hooks I hung whatever I need not cook the minute I got home from Aix: white onions in a crocheted bag, two kilos of long purple eggplants that not even a bee could sting, a basket of small, satin-skinned potatoes. On the old piano I would put a tray of red tomatoes, which I had placed gently, bottoms up, with some soft ones, already doomed for tomorrow, to be eaten tonight, even though they had all been firm and greenish a few hours before. I would do the same with a tray of peaches and apricots, and then cover them against the midges.

Baskets of green peas and one of beans I put upon the table in the dining room, with pans to catch them when they were shelled and de-strung by whoever passed by. It was a house rule, and since everybody talked and sat and drank and worked in that big white room, as well as eating there when we were not out under the pine trees on the terrace, it seemed a pleasant and nearly automatic thing to prepare for cooking whatever was set out for that.

In the little kitchen, I put things away as fast as I could. If I had bought meat, it must be prepared for cooking at once, or at best kept in the minute frigidaire overnight. (In winter, of course, things could be thoroughly wrapped and put on a window ledge or into a wire cooler, but winter is not long in that country, and the rats and half-wild farm cats are very clever about getting around such casual arrangements.)

Then I would pack the sweet fresh butter into a crock

and put it on the old piano in a bowl of water. I washed the strawberries and cherries tenderly and put them, too, in heavy bowls in the buttery, to be eaten that day. Salads I stripped of their bad leaves and soaked for a few minutes in a dishpan, and then shook out and wrapped in a towel, to be eaten within twenty-four hours. Sometimes I could store clean curly endive or chicory and the coarser lettuces in cellophane bags for a little longer, but not in summer. It was fine, in winter, to have plenty of good Belgian endive – so easy to clean, to store, to serve in many ways.

It takes little time to learn the tricks of any new kitchen if it is a question of survival, and after only a few days at L'Harmas I knew which pans had bad handles, which skillets heated unevenly, which burners on the stove were not worth bothering to light. I knew where I was going to put bottle caps and broken corks and empty anchovy tins, all separate, and what I was going to do about garbage, and where I would hang the dish towels. I also knew where not to trip on a loose tile, and how to keep ants out of the honey jar forever. I remembered a lot of tricks from the last time in Provence, at Le Tholonet.

I remembered that in summer it is dangerous to make any kind of soup and hope to keep some of it for the next day; it will send off the sweet, sickly death smell in only a few hours, even from a jar in the frigidaire. And I remembered how to stew fruits lightly, to keep them overnight for a cool bowl for breakfast or lunch instead of having to eat them all and immediately. Once more I was washing everything fast in pure water from the well instead of the tap, to keep my people from the queasy gripes and grumbles that can plague countryfolk and that used to frighten pioneer American mothers with names like 'summer complaint' and 'fruit fever.'

Soon I would go without thinking to the little icebox and that cool dark buttery, about twice a day, to sniff with my curious nose and to discard ruthlessly what it always hurt me to waste: a bowl of berries delicately veiled with a fine grey fuzz that was not there an hour ago, three more rotten tomatoes that were firm and fine last night. I would lift the lid from a pot of leftover ratatouille – was it really all right, or did I catch a whiff, a hint, of death and decay in it? A deep sniff might make me decide that it would be safe to bring it again to the boil, beat it well with some more olive oil, and chill it to be eaten cold with fresh bread for supper, before an omelet. There might be one lamb chop left. It would not be good by noon. I would eat it cold for a secret breakfast, with a glass of red wine, after the family had scattered. Tomorrow would be market again.

In winter, when alone, I ate by the fire on the hearth of the living-dining room. In spring, I carried my plate and glass into the new warmth of sunlight on the terrace, ankle-deep in wild flowers and a hundred tender grasses. In summer, I sat by the bowed shutters in the dining room; dim to baffle the flies, cool already against the blaze of white dusty heat, vibrating with the love call of the *cigales*. In the autumn, I walked a little away from roof and room to the meadows turning sere, to the pine woods past the wheat field, and I put my back against a tree and looked north toward the Mont Ste. Victoire, rising so arrogant and harsh above the curling foreground.

I would think of what I must buy the next day, and load into the baskets, and then sort and store and serve forth in the order of Nature itself: first freshness, then flavor and ripeness, and then decay. And always there were the needs of the people who must live from Nature, and learn to do so to the best of all their powers and not die from the traps that she can lay for them, especially in this ancient teeming land.

It was a good way to live.

Love Letter to an Empty Shell

It was probably Jonathan Swift, of all the poets and preachers who have considered the oyster, who said most succinctly that it was a bold man that first ate one. I myself have felt only a quick, conditioned qualm at 17, and have continued boldly through all the shellfish, from abalones to winkles. In between I have savored clams, cockles, mussels, scallops, sea urchins and a few other unidentified briny tidbits. (I have also chewed less happily once on the rubbery flesh of sea snails, in Les Saintes-Maries-de-la-Mer, and have drunk the sandy delicate broth from *coquinas*, dug by hand along the Southern California beaches in less polluted days.)

It was a sad waste of time to wait almost two decades before my first oyster, but I know that if I had been born to different parents and in a different clime, I would have thrived on shellfish of every taste and texture from my first days. Very young people, even the newborn, eat raw shellfish and drink their breedy juices without question: 'protoplasm to protoplasm,' as Samuel Butler once wrote in a rumination about eating and loving and hating and so forth.

I was raised by Anglo-Saxons, who for several generations had worked their way unerringly from Britain to the East Coast of America to the Far West, with lengthy stopovers on the middle plains for reproductive purposes.

Any atavistic memories of cracking open an oyster or steaming a clam had long since been dimmed in them by the time I appeared. We lived in placid ignorance at the edge of the fruitful Pacific, until one night at boarding school I emptied the first of what became, through decades, enough shells of the edible *Ostrea* to form a solid bridge between almost any two given points: Long Beach and Catalina Island, Toulon and Porquerolles . . .

It is true that I was subtly and unwittingly led into this continuing hunger by an occasional almost furtive feast of mussels during the summers in Laguna Beach, while my mother, inland, had more children. The gathering and steaming of the shellfish by my father was arduous, exciting and something we kept quiet about, since they could not possibly have been enjoyed fully in the sedate dining room ruled over by Grandmother. Eating them involved drippings, slurpings, moans of pleasure, animal sighs of repletion.

I do not remember eating mussels alive in Laguna. We always steamed them on a bed of sea grass in an old oilcan over a good bed of coals. As soon as they opened, we ate them from full bowls brought at a run from the backyard to the table with a dishpan in the middle for the shells. Some of us ate them one by one, right to the mouth from the blue-black pearly scoop, and some pulled out little piles of the coral lumps and ate them with a spoon. There were halves of lemon, a pitcher of melted butter and a good loaf of bread. It was not at all the proper sort of meal we had at home.

I started eating *live* mussels when I was perhaps 20, in Dijon. Mussels were looked down on then, at least in Burgundy, and were used mostly for 'made dishes.' But there was a place called Crespin that usually had a couple of baskets of them out on the sidewalk in the winter months, along with one or two of small clams, and dozens of oyster cases – all dripping saltwater from the seaweeds they were packed with and sending out a fine masculine smell.

That was in 1929. The prices and the choice were much more varied than now, when even at Prunier in Paris there is only a skinny handful of kinds to choose from, all costing pure gold. If we were in funds, we ate Belons, then Claires or Marennes. If we felt pinchy, we ate Portugaises Vertes, which were not as refined in taste then as they seem now. If we were really low financially but still felt festive, we would eat mussels. No matter how broke, we always saved the price of at least two gulps to give to the oysterman – a huge gray and blue and purple monument with almost unrecognizable hands like mashed hams, who stood out on the sidewalk in the meanest weather, warmed by some inner merriment and an occasional *marc*.

Oyster eaters are almost always in full possession of their faculties, gastronomical and otherwise. An oyster is one of the very few things a human being will eat alive, as well as one of the simplest complexes of chemistry and nature, so that pregnant women, feverish or peaked children, dying presidents and even popes, have been nourished, soothed and revivified by the savoring of two or a hundred fresh, succulent bivalves. And all the rest of us, great and puny, have we not been comforted and picked up in our spirits by oysters from a corner stall, or a rich stew from a bowl?

There has long been an idea basically hopeful, that oysters contribute to sexual strength. I have never had to put the theory to the test. I think that anyone who eats oysters before making love is enjoying a gastric reprieve, belly working happily on essential and easily absorbed elements, so that the rest of the body is not only freed from digesting heavy sauces and so on, but is stimulated to more activity in other regions. In other words, I doubt strongly that oysters have any aphrodisiacal values, but know they are eminently easy to absorb for strength and nourishment!

From what I have read, the Greeks and the Celts made the best use of oysters in the ancient world, except, of course, for the Chinese. All of these cultures in somewhat modified forms still show respect and even love for the mollusk. The Chinese, largely because of storage problems, invented a delicious seasoning sauce that can still be bought in bottles, a noble forerunner of Mrs. Beeton's Oyster Ketchup, much as the Roman *garum*, in a far less dignified way, sired our current variations on the Worcestershire theme.

Thackeray stated firmly, and to my regret if not his own, 'I was never much of an oyster eater, nor can I relish them *in naturalibus* as some do, but require a quantity of sauces, lemons, cayenne peppers, bread and butter, and so forth, to render them palatable.' Myself, I feel that an oyster in its best state needs nothing more than to be opened for me! To do this so that none of the vital juices spill anywhere but down my greedy throat takes a skill that so far I have had little need to develop. Once the shell is in my hand, I am an adept at emptying it, so that the whole contents slip past my palate after a voluptous bit of chewing, and of pressing them against the roof of my mouth for extra sensations. This simple rite can be performed anywhere, although a Delaware lady once told me that it was considered vulgar to chew an oyster at a dinner party or in a good restaurant. Perhaps street barrows and bars are best?

There are many ways to tell if an oyster is alive and therefore fresh. It is believed, and probably with reason, that the main muscle should be flat or even sunken, since if it bulges upward like a beer belly, the oyster is either very tired or is defunct. The best way, for me, is to touch with my finger or a fork the delicate flanges or 'mantle' on the longer side of the shell, or to breathe upon it. If the oyster is alive, it will cringe back. This is simple, if perhaps cruel. But the whole process comes down to that, if one credits a mollusk with the ability to suffer.

There are many refinements to downing a raw oyster, given one's callousness to this somewhat spiritual problem. Oysters can be chewed at will and swallowed at leisure. Or they can be gulped straight down, especially if doused in Thackeray's fiery disguises.

Some people like to shake a bath of flavored vinegar on a raw oyster in its shell, or squeeze a little fresh lemon over it, perhaps to see if its flanges will pull back and perhaps to make it less blatantly protoplasmic. Some people go even further and mask it freely from a bottle of 'hot sauce,' a local liquor found from one part of the planet to another, always based on the wildest form of available pepper: cayenne, chili, red pimiento. It may be that these conditioned reflexes stem from a mistaken idea of hygiene. Better to choke down a bad oyster than none at all? Then there are slightly more merciful mixtures called dab sauces along the Carolina coast and, as far as I know, not even named in New Orleans. There are bottles of the 'makings' on oyster bars and tables: catsup, sometimes Worcestershire, Tabasco or a local copy of it and, in Louisiana, always horseradish. People mix their own poison in little pepper cups with wooden paddles. Such teasers are guaranteed to kill any flabby brackishness of a questionable shellfish, as well as all subtlety and flavor of the freshest, finest oyster ever raked or scooped or dug or even *bought*. But I am too occupied with my own way of enjoyment to bother about the benighted state of my fellow addicts.

Perhaps it is more merciful, to the human palate if not the oysters, to kill them outright by cooking them. This is an alternative dictated by early inadequacies in chilling and preservation, and to anyone who prefers the raw ones it is a basic shame. Cooked oysters can be very good, though. Depending on the treatment, such fare can be the second-best of both beautiful worlds. A real buff can down a dozen fresh from the shell at a place like Felix's in New Orleans, for instance, attend to whatever he has to do, and then face another collection of them at Galatoire's for lunch or dinner or supper, artfully simmered in a dainty thin broth in a bowl, or grilled with bacon on a skewer, or lying on pillows of puréed herbs in the shells, all perfumed with herbsaint and suchlike.

I firmly believe that almost anybody in his right mind and body can face oysters, both raw and cooked, at least twice a day if not oftener, and emerge the better for it.

In France, one of the leading nations for centuries in the consumption of them, they are preferred cool and fresh and raw, although *Larousse Gastronomique* gives more than 30 excellent recipes for cooking them. I have turned usually red-faced Burgundians pale by describing a good oyster stew. '*Quelle horreur*,' they have muttered: all this senseless murder, and *milk*, too! This is still, to my mind, however, the best way to eat shellfish if they must be hot. A stew should be made fast, from the best oysters, the best milk and butter, the best paprika. Fortunately it can also be very commendable when made of pasteurized half-and-half, margarine and those oysters in glass jars that are labeled 'Fresh' but last a suspiciously long time in supermarket refrigerators. I have yet to try to compose a hopefully honest stew with the canned kind, but suspect that they should be chopped, being fairly tough. This of course changes the whole classical allure: a proper stew must be creamy in color, with *whole* plump tender oysters floating generously in it.

There are many recipes for a bisque, though, using oysters chopped, minced, ground and even blendered, and when I re-read them I wonder why I do not make them oftener, for they are delicious when hot, and near-perfection served very cold on a summer day. And next to the stew and the bisque, in my private primer, comes the old-fashioned 'scallop,' a crumby, buttery dish so succulent-simple that it has its own elegance. (Big oysters can be chopped for it.) As is often the case, such homely recipes are at their most trustworthy in the traditional kitchen manuals, from Mrs. Beeton through Larousse to Mrs. Rombauer, and make for pleasurable armchair gastronomy as well.

Clams take a somewhat smaller role in the lexicons. Like oysters, they are usually best eaten fresh and whole. They can turn very tough when cooked carelessly, so are often chopped or sliced thin. Canned minced clams are a basic part of a good pantry, to my mind, and recipes for using them are tantalizing, especially when collected for charitable purposes by the ladies of a church in Maine or Virginia, or even for plain public relations by a road-side clam house in California – delicious, if not infallible!

And mussels, smoked or in brine, are good from cans, if one must live in full frustration on a coast condemned by the health authorities for its high population of dino-flagellates as well as its increasingly general nastiness. And frozen scallops are delicious in too many ways to count. Even canned abalone can be coped with successfully. It is possible that sea snails and winkles may be available in preserves of one kind or another – in Holland or Norway if not here. Perhaps the sea urchin, that most delicate of all shellfish, is the only one left firmly inviolate?

It would be fun to write about the first time a shellfish freak like me ate each new find: an urchin pulled deep off a rock in a sinister *calanque* between Toulon and Cassis, and the boatman breaking off some of the spines and thumbing out the guts and then offering it courteously to me to suck, while pointing out the scars along the edges of the narrow canyon where the enemy submarines had rubbed not long before; cold boiled winkles and a pin to jab them with, in a small pub in Liverpool, while the tides stayed too low to lift our freighter out of port; cherry-stones, small and crisp, at Keen's English Chop House in New York, in 1941, when the world-of-the-moment seemed to be whirling out of focus except for that cool nutty taste.

There is one fishy preparation I have never eaten, and that is a pickled oyster, but here and now – and in a pitifully shell-free environment – I feel that I can best survive such possible challenges as a pickled oyster might be by remembering past pleasures, and sipping an occasional glass of an evocative white wine. Yes, about a year ago, there were the Belons and the clams and the mussels and the urchins I was eating in Marseilles. And a few months ago there were perhaps a dozen, dozen oysters in six days, in every state of brief life and honor-able death, in the pubs and palaces of New Orleans.

How can I know what may lie ahead? As long as it contains a soothing of my insatiable delight in shellfish. I can hardly wait.

Wine is Life

I can no more think of my own life without thinking of wine and wines and where they grew for me and why I drank them when I did and why I picked the grapes and where I opened the oldest procurable bottles, and all that, than I can remember living before I breathed. In other words, wine *is* life, and my life and wine are inextricable. And the saving grace of all wine's many graces, probably, is that it can never be dull. It is only the people who try to sing about it who may sound flat. But wine is an older thing than we are, and is forgiving of even the most boring explanations of its *élan vital*.

In some ways there is nothing much more encouraging about man's stumbling progress than his growing deftness in making good wine better and then getting it to the mouths and minds of more people. On the other hand, perhaps it has lost some of its mystery and luster in its new availability. The leap from a high priest's sacramental flagon on a marble altar to the plastic container in a motel icebox is shorter than we care to ponder.

Myself, I am glad that people almost everywhere can find potable and honest wines more easily than they used to, even in supermarkets. It was impossible to buy anything alcoholic in Whittier, where we went when I was about four, because it was a town founded by and for the Quaker way of life. My father Rex respected this aim, but as a non-Quaker he did not subscribe to it, and some of the best times of my young life were spent driving into the beautiful hills and hidden quiet valleys of southern California with him to buy house-wines. I loved the cold smell of wine cellars as much as I did the fine whiff of ink and fresh paper at the daily NEWS.

It never surprised me that the ranchers always seemed glad when we drove up their roads in our open Model-T. The women would put tumblers and a long loaf of their last baking, and cheese or a dry sausage, on the kitchen table or under the grape arbor 'out back.' When the men came with two or three bottles from the old barn or hillside cellar where the casks were stored, they would eat and try the wines and talk. The women and I stayed carefully apart, and I was always given a seed-cake or a piece of bread and jam. Finally the jugs Rex had brought along were filled, and sometimes he took older bottles for special days ahead, and we drove away gently so as not to jiggle them too much.

The wines were probably crude and dirty, compared to what we can buy everywhere today. They were unpasteurized, unfiltered, unfined, not made to last long. Although I know that now and then I was given some at the little ranches well watered to a sickly pink, I cannot remember anything except that I loved the bouncy rides and the fair countryside, and my father for taking me along with him.

My anglophile mother liked to serve heavy brownish sherries occasionally with desserts, and I was always given a ceremonial sniff or sip, which I still associate with the communion wine I did not taste until after I was twelve, of course in our small Episcopal church. By then, Prohibition had been in effect for over a year, and we were firmly known in Whittier as the only so-called religious group in town that deliberately flouted the law and served 'liquor' from its altar rail. This was, I learned later, because my father, as a respected vestryman, refused flatly to invest in the barrel-washings that were then called sacramental wines, and managed somehow to have a comparatively fine imported sherry sipped from the St. Matthias chalice. It always made our empty stomachs rumble at the Early Service, but at least it was decent stuff, and although Rex himself only went to church on Christmas and Easter mornings, he felt it his duty to protect his elected brethren from what he mildly referred to as Volstead Swill.

Until 1919 and Prohibition, though, I really enjoyed beer more than I did wine as a day-to-day tipple. Before World War I, I went often with Father to Anaheim, where we filled the back of the Ford with fresh bottles from two or three of the small German breweries there. As I now understand it, this was almost as easy in southern California as it had been in Albion, Michigan, where my parents had run a smaller newspaper than the NEWS and had started a family. There, and then in the little Quaker town, my father put the paper to bed by about three o'clock, six afternoons a week, and walked home to sit on the front porch or by the fire and drink a bottle of beer with Mother. And I got to carry the empty bottle and two glasses to the kitchen and tip back the last few delicious drops of bitter dead brew. (If for no other good reason, this early sampling taught me the mighty difference between real beer and the pale foamy water we now mass-produce in the United States.)

All during Prohibition we kept two decanters on the dining room sideboard, half filled with fairly good sherry and a mediocre port, mostly used to make an occasional Tipsy Parson when our teetotaller grandmother was out of town. We never drank at the table when she was in residence, out of respect, but that was a time of frequent church gatherings for her, so that almost any birthday or fiesta, sacred or profane, meant a good bottle on the table. We children always had a sip or two in our own glasses but seldom drank them. And Cresta Blanca is the only wine name left in my mind, for a round rich red. The others were unlabeled, from a little vineyard off the Workman Mill Road, or Futelli's over near Cucamonga, or Old Man Johnson's back of Corona. They had to be honest to be good, and good meant *drinkable*.

We moved down Painter Avenue and into the country when I was eleven, and as money flowed faster in the decade before the Crash of 1929, the family served dependable bootleg liquor to their friends, and the wines came oftener and tasted more exciting. The two decanters still stayed on the sideboard, and it was understood that if we young ones wanted to drink in our own home, Father would gladly offer what he had to our guests, as long as they knew how to behave. We never accepted this tacit invitation, but as a clear result of it and of our complete lack of any need to find forbidden fruits, my younger sister and I emerged from our Prohibition teens with our livers intact and our palates unscarred by the poisons our dates carried in flat silver flasks to all the football games and dances. The flesh-warm booze was literally impossible for us to swallow, because we already knew what good drink tasted like, and we were young and healthy and had no need for extra stimulants. Other girls told us we must drink with our dates or have none, but we danced blandly past the Crash of '29 and into the Depression, learning a lot about the drinking patterns of our times, but always backed by what we had been taught unwittingly since our youngest days. There was good wine if we cared to look for it, or good beer – gin – whiskey – brandy. And the best was none *too* good!

In 1929, I started to learn more seriously about wine-making and winetasting when I married and went to live in France, mostly in Burgundy, for three years. We were lucky to live there with the Ollagniers first and then the Rigoulots, who were as different as two middle-class French families can be but who shared a genuine zeal for learning how to live intensely. They used all their physical senses steadily and deliberately, like musicians or surgeons training their fingers, and they studied and talked and polished all their wits like artisans honing their tools.

When Paul Ollagnier, a municipal architect, had to inspect the attic beams in an old château down the Côte d'Or near Gevrey-Chambertin, for instance, he took us along, and we saw how to use the little silver *tâte-vins* and stand like polite awed sheep, in the cellars or courtyards, while the men went through their long obligatory tastings after the business at hand was over. The smell of ice-cold stone and wine and mildew was good. We were *learning*, with every cell and pore in our young minds and bodies.

On Sundays the Ollagniers took us on rough endless walks with the Club Alpin, and we ate and drank our ways through endless enormous meals in village cafés that seemed to live for our annual treks, and then we snoozed for endless train-rides back to Dijon and bed and the next week's classes. And all week we discussed with the family the dishes and wines we'd absorbed on Sunday, as if they were Corneille or Voltaire or the *futur indicatif* of the verb 'to understand.'

M. Ollagnier had a cousin in Belley in the Ain, who occasionally sent him a gamey pâté or some long-necked bottles of pale rosé or straw-wine from his vineyard farm, so I learned about Brillat-Savarin's country and started then and there my 'continuing delight' in that old man's good company. I read the Ollagnier copy of his Physiology of Taste and was as surprised then as I still am that few Frenchmen knew of it.

And then the Rigoulots rented us along with the Dijon house and for many more months taught us a completely sensual and almost hectic approach to the pleasures of the table, as compared to the more academic detachment of the architect and his pianist-wife.

We ate too much and too heavily and drank fine bottles every day instead of on Sundays, as we hurtled with the passionate, desperate people toward their family ruin and then World War II. They had once been very rich, with a fine cellar, mostly of Burgundian and Alsatian vintages, and by then my husband and I knew more about what and why we were drinking. The good bottles and the delicate fine dishes and all the urgency of disintegration mixed into a strange dream for a time. What is left is sometimes sad in my heart, but always good, *sans reproche*.

Back again in California, there was the end of Prohibition, a forgotten blight while we'd been away. There was no extra money anywhere, so the new watery beer and the dregs of bootlegged booze were easy to forgo. Now and then a few of us would 'chip in' for a gallon of young but decent red wine, and eat bread and maybe cheese and talk all night, and plan glowing beautiful exciting futures as the jug emptied. We never felt like clichés-in-Time, which of course we were, politics and poverty and gallantry and all . . .

And since my first years and Father's sure insistence that there could always be good wine if it were looked for, I have found it and not bothered with anything else. By now the skill of growing and making it in California has progressed so far that I feel more secure than ever in my lifelong pursuit. Of course there will be shoddy bottles forever, because of the shoddy men forever born to fill and market them. But they cannot harm me, because I have never stopped learning how to tell the true from the false, with at least six of my five allotted senses. Any good winemaker keeps on learning, too, and this collection of some of the reasons for doing so, and the ways devised to assure that, would give heart to my own first teacher, Rex.

He took a dim view of Brotherly Love, the Immaculate Conception, and Prohibition, according to critics as disparate as my mother and the County Boxing Commission, among others. He smoked cigarettes, mostly hand-rolled with Bull Durham, and pipe-tobacco until he lost his bite with dentures in his late years. He probably downed more than his share of drinkin-likka, as a newspaperman. He should have had a palate like well-tanned buffalo hide. But I never saw him smoke when honest wine was nearby, or falter in his first long silent appraisal of it, whether he was in a rancher's dim barn up in the California foothills, or in a Swiss vintner's cellar, or in a fine restaurant any place.

He was not my only teacher in this 'appreciation course' that I shall continue to attend as long as I am conscient, but certainly he was the shaper, the power behind what I always feel when I know that I am drinking a good wine and that I may soon drink another. *Prosit*, to him and all such mentors!

GREAT FOOD

BUFFALO CAKE AND INDIAN PUDDING

Dr A. W. Chase

TRAVELLING PHYSICIAN, SALESMAN, author and self-made man, Dr Chase dispensed remedies all over America during the late nineteenth century, collecting recipes and domestic tips from the people he met along the way. His self-published books became celebrated US bestsellers and were the household bibles of their day.

Containing recipes for American-style treats, such as Boston cream cakes, Kentucky corn dodgers and pumpkin pie, as well as genial advice on baking bread and testing whether a cake is cooked, this is a treasure trove of culinary wisdom from the homesteads of a still rural, pioneering United States.

GREAT FOOD

EVERLASTING SYLLABUB AND THE ART OF CARVING

Hannah Glasse

WRITING FOR DOMESTIC SERVANTS in a conversational, accessible way, eighteenth-century housewife Hannah Glasse disapproved of French terminology and fussiness, instead favouring simple dishes that are still cooked today – a preference that has earned her the reputation of being 'the first domestic goddess'.

With recipes for rice pudding, beef rump, barbecued pork, trifle and even the first recipe in Britain for 'curry the Indian way', as well as tips for choosing your ingredients and cures for the bite of a mad dog, this is an elegant and economical collection of recipes and housekeeping tips to save any homemaker 'a great deal of trouble'.

'The first domestic goddess'
CLARISSA DICKSON-WRIGHT

GREAT FOOD

A LITTLE DINNER
BEFORE THE PLAY

Agnes Jekyll

WHETHER EXTOLLING THE MERITS of a cheerful breakfast tray, conjuring up a winter picnic of figs and mulled wine, sharing delicious Tuscan recipes, or suggesting a last-minute pre-theatre dinner, the sparkling writings of the society hostess and philanthropist Agnes Jekyll describe food for every imaginable occasion and mood.

Originally published in *The Times* in the early 1920s, these divinely witty and brilliantly observed pieces are still loved today for their warmth and friendly advice and, with their emphasis on fresh, simple, stylish dishes, were years ahead of their time.

'Beautifully written, sparkling, witty and knowing,
an absolute delight to read'
INDIA KNIGHT

GREAT FOOD

EXCITING FOOD FOR
SOUTHERN TYPES

Pellegrino Artusi

PELLEGRINO ARTUSI is the original icon of
Italian cookery, whose legendary 1891 book *Science
in the Kitchen and the Art of Eating Well* defined its
national cuisine and is still a bestseller today.

He was also a passionate gastronome, renowned
host and brilliant raconteur, who filled his books with
tasty recipes and rumbustious anecdotes. From an
unfortunate incident regarding minestrone in Livorno
and a proud defence of the humble meat loaf, to
digressions on the unusual history of ice-cream, the
side-effects of cabbage and the Florentines' weak
constitutions, these writings brim with gossip, good
cheer and an inexhaustible zest for life.

'The fountainhead of modern Italian cookery'
GASTRONOMICA

GREAT FOOD

A TASTE OF THE SUN

Elizabeth David

LEGENDARY COOK AND WRITER Elizabeth David
changed the way Britain ate, introducing a postwar nation
to the sun-drenched delights of the Mediterranean, and
bringing new flavours and aromas such as garlic,
wine and olive oil into its kitchens.

This mouthwatering selection of her writings and
recipes embraces the richness of French and Italian cuisine,
from earthy cassoulets to the simplest spaghetti, as well as
evoking the smell of buttered toast, the colours of foreign
markets and the pleasures of picnics. Rich with anecdote,
David's writing is defined by a passion for good, authentic,
well-balanced food that still inspires chefs today.

*'Above all, Elizabeth David's books
make you want to cook'*
TERENCE CONRAN

GREAT FOOD

MURDER IN THE KITCHEN
Alice B. Toklas

IN THIS MEMOIR-TURNED-COOKBOOK,
Alice B. Toklas describes her life with partner Gertrude
Stein and their famed Paris salon, which entertained the
great avant-garde and literary figures of their day.

With dry wit and characteristic understatement Toklas
ponders the ethics of killing a carp in her kitchen before
stuffing it with chestnuts; decorating a fish to amuse
Picasso at lunch; and travelling across France during the
First World War in an old delivery truck, gathering
local recipes along the way. She includes a friend's
playful recipe for 'haschiche fudge', which
promises 'brilliant storms of laughter and
ecstatic reveries', much like her book.

*'It will be the fiercest Francophobe who can read
Alice's recipes and not hanker for a taste'*
TIME

····· GREAT FOOD ·····

A MIDDLE EASTERN FEAST
Claudia Roden

AWARD-WINNING FOOD WRITER Claudia Roden
revolutionized Western attitudes to the cuisines of the
Middle East with her bestselling *Book of Middle Eastern
Food*. Introducing millions to enticing new scents and
flavours, her intensely personal, passionate writings
conveyed an age-old tradition of family eating and shared
memory. This selection includes recipes for tagines from
Morocco, rice from Iran, peasant soup from ancient
Egypt and kofta from Armenia, as well as discussions of
spices, market bargaining, childhood memories of Cairo
and the etiquette of tea drinking; evoking not only a
cuisine but an entire way of life.

*'Roden's great gift is to conjure up not just a cuisine
but the culture from which it springs'*
NIGELLA LAWSON

····· GREAT FOOD ·····

RECIPES AND LESSONS FROM A DELICIOUS COOKING REVOLUTION

Alice Waters

A CHAMPION OF ORGANIC, locally produced and seasonal food and founder of acclaimed Californian restaurant Chez Panisse, Alice Waters has recently been awarded the *Légion d'honneur* in France for her contributions to food culture. In this book, she explores the simplest of dishes in the most delicious of ways, with fresh, sustainable ingredients a must, even encouraging cooks to plant their own garden.

From orange and olive salad to lemon curd and ginger snaps, Waters constantly emphasizes the joys and ease of cooking with local, fresh food, whether in soups, salads or sensual, classic desserts.

'*Waters is a legend*'
JAY RAYNER

GREAT FOOD

FROM ABSINTHE TO ZEST
An Alphabet for Food Lovers

Alexandre Dumas

AS WELL AS BEING THE AUTHOR OF *The Three Musketeers*, Alexandre Dumas was also an enthusiastic gourmand and expert cook. His *Grand Dictionnaire de Cuisine*, published in 1873, is an encyclopaedic collection of ingredients, recipes and anecdotes, from Absinthe to Zest via cake, frogs' legs, oysters, roquefort and vanilla.

Included here are recipes for bamboo pickle and strawberry omelette, advice on cooking all manner of beast from bear to kangaroo – as well as delightful digressions into how a fig started a war and whether truffles really increase ardour – brought together in a witty and gloriously eccentric culinary compendium.

'From the great French novelist and obsessive gourmet. The cook book as literature'
NORMAN SPINRAD

GREAT  FOOD

THROUGHOUT the history of civilization, food has been
livelihood, status symbol, entertainment – and passion.
The twenty fine food writers here, reflecting on different
cuisines from across the centuries and around the globe, have
influenced each other and continue to influence us today,
opening the door to the wonders of every kitchen.